Planning for the Aftermath

Assessing Options for U.S. Strategy
Toward Russia After the Ukraine War

SAMUEL CHARAP AND MIRANDA PRIEBE

NATIONAL SECURITY RESEARCH DIVISION

For more information on this publication, visit **www.rand.org/t/RRA2510-2**.

About RAND

The RAND Corporation is a research organization that develops solutions to public policy challenges to help make communities throughout the world safer and more secure, healthier and more prosperous. RAND is nonprofit, nonpartisan, and committed to the public interest. To learn more about RAND, visit www.rand.org.

Research Integrity

Our mission to help improve policy and decisionmaking through research and analysis is enabled through our core values of quality and objectivity and our unwavering commitment to the highest level of integrity and ethical behavior. To help ensure our research and analysis are rigorous, objective, and nonpartisan, we subject our research publications to a robust and exacting quality-assurance process; avoid both the appearance and reality of financial and other conflicts of interest through staff training, project screening, and a policy of mandatory disclosure; and pursue transparency in our research engagements through our commitment to the open publication of our research findings and recommendations, disclosure of the source of funding of published research, and policies to ensure intellectual independence. For more information, visit www.rand.org/about/principles.

RAND's publications do not necessarily reflect the opinions of its research clients and sponsors.

Published by the RAND Corporation, Santa Monica, Calif.
© 2024 RAND Corporation
RAND® is a registered trademark.

Library of Congress Cataloging-in-Publication Data is available for this publication.
ISBN: 978-1-9774-1283-6

Cover image: MasterSergeant/Adobe Stock.

Limited Print and Electronic Distribution Rights

About This Report

As the fighting in Ukraine continues, it has been difficult for U.S. policymakers to look beyond wartime decisions and consider the long-term postwar U.S. approach toward Russia. Great powers' choices at the end of a war tend to have far-reaching and lasting consequences, so although the conflict is not over, the United States should begin considering its options. In this report, we offer a framework to help policymakers evaluate strategic options in different postwar contexts. We apply this framework to generate four alternative futures for the postwar decade and highlight their implications for U.S. interests.

This report builds on earlier analysis of the war's trajectory and U.S. wartime policy in Samuel Charap and Miranda Priebe, *Avoiding a Long War: U.S. Policy and the Trajectory of the Russia-Ukraine Conflict*, PE-A2510-1, RAND Corporation, 2023.

RAND Center for Analysis of U.S. Grand Strategy

Funding for this research was provided by a generous gift from Peter Richards, a longtime RAND supporter and member of the RAND Global and Emerging Risks Advisory Board, and conducted within the RAND Center for Analysis of U.S. Grand Strategy. The center's mission is to inform the debate about the U.S. role in the world by more clearly specifying new approaches to U.S. grand strategy, evaluating the logic of different approaches, and identifying the trade-offs each option creates. Initial funding for the center was provided by a seed grant from the Stand Together Trust. Ongoing funding comes from RAND Corporation supporters and from foundations and philanthropists.

The center is an initiative of the International Security and Defense Policy Program of the RAND National Security Research Division (NSRD). NSRD conducts research and analysis for the Office of the Secretary of Defense, the U.S. Intelligence Community, the U.S. State Department, allied foreign governments, and foundations.

For more information on the RAND Center for Analysis of U.S. Grand Strategy, see www.rand.org/nsrd/isdp/grand-strategy or contact the center director (contact information is provided on the webpage).

Acknowledgments

We thank Peter Richards for his deep engagement with the research and thoughtful suggestions and questions that helped us improve the analysis. We also thank Joe Haberman, Clara de Lataillade, Mina Pollman, Alexandra Stark, and Gabrielle Tarini for assistance with background research, as well as Keith Darden, Jeremy Shapiro, Howard Shatz, and Tobias Systma for consulting with us. We appreciate John Godges's help with an earlier draft, figure design by Kristen Meadows, and editing by Rachel Ostrow. Finally, we benefited from thoughtful comments from reviewers Karl Mueller (RAND Corporation) and William Wohlforth (Dartmouth College).

Summary

Issue

U.S. policy choices at the end of past wars have had enduring consequences. Although there is no end in sight to the Russia-Ukraine war at the time of this writing in late 2023, U.S. policymakers should begin considering postwar Russia strategy now. To facilitate these considerations, in this report we review U.S. strategic options and the trade-offs that different choices create for U.S. interests.

Approach

We address this issue through an alternative futures analysis. Because U.S. policy toward a major rival is never designed or implemented in a vacuum, we begin by considering the postwar setting that the United States may face. We develop two ideal-type postwar *worlds*, as defined by the outcome of the war and the character of the broader international environment: a *less favorable* world and a *more favorable* world. Next, we propose two ideal-type options for postwar U.S. strategy toward Russia, which we call a *hardline* approach and a *less hardline* approach. Finally, we consider how each strategic option would play out in each world over the course of the decade after the war ends, yielding four alternative futures. We draw on the history of U.S.-Russia relations and the literatures on rivalries, interstate conflict, and alliances to describe key dynamics in each future and assess the implications of each future for U.S. interests.

These futures are not intended to predict how the postwar decade will unfold. However, such an analysis can help policymakers anticipate the impact of wartime policies on the postwar environment and the trade-offs associated with different strategic choices.

Observations

Several observations stem from the analysis of the four alternative futures.

A longer, more violent war would have long-term and likely irreversible adverse consequences for U.S. interests. For example, a longer war would have negative economic effects on the United States, its allies, and Ukraine, regardless of postwar U.S. strategy.

The United States may be able to influence the conflict outcome to promote its long-term interests. The United States has policy options to, for example, encourage Russia and Ukraine to pursue a ceasefire sooner rather than later.

U.S. policy during and after the war can reduce the risk of Russia-Ukraine conflict recurrence. For example, using U.S. influence to encourage a nearer-term end to the war would likely leave Ukraine in a better position to deter a future Russian invasion. The United States can promote a more robust ceasefire that could reduce the risk of events along the line of conflict escalating to another war. Washington can also encourage Kyiv to adopt a military posture optimized for defense rather than continuing to focus on capabilities for retaking Russian-held territory. Doing so could limit Kyiv's ability to liberate occupied areas but would make it harder for Russia to take more territory, increasing Kyiv's ability to deter Moscow from restarting the war.

A hardline postwar U.S. strategy in Europe could make conflict with Russia more—not less—likely. The war has both weakened Russia's military and demonstrated that the North Atlantic Treaty Organization (NATO) has a strong deterrent against Russian attacks on allies, even as allies aid Ukraine's war effort. Therefore, hardline U.S. policies in the postwar context—such as a further buildup in Europe—are unlikely to be necessary to effectively deter an opportunistic Russian attack on a NATO member-state. Moreover, such policies could increase the risk of other pathways to conflict with Russia, such as war brought about by possible Kremlin misperception of U.S. intentions.

This assessment assumes that U.S.-Russia conflict would result from Moscow's assertive responses to hardline policies, not opportunistic aggression. Our assessment about conflict risk resulting from a hardline strategy assumes that Russia's risk tolerance remains the same as today and that the Kremlin responds assertively to hardline U.S. policies, provoking spirals of hostility that make conflict more likely. If either of these assumptions are wrong, then a hardline strategy could reduce the risk of conflict.

Closer Russia-China ties may be irreversible. Before the war, Beijing and Moscow's ties were driven by a shared concern about U.S. power and foreign policy; relations have deepened further during the war. In the postwar setting, a hardline U.S. policy toward Russia could create more incentives for greater Russia-China cooperation. A moderately less hardline approach, such as the one we consider, would avoid creating such additional incentives; but it would be unlikely to alter the underlying suspicions of the United States that sustain the relationship.

Some postwar divides within NATO might prove more significant for the United States than others. After the war, such allies as France, Italy, and Germany may see a hardline U.S. approach toward Russia as excessively provocative. Conversely, some Eastern European allies would likely oppose a less hardline U.S. approach under most circumstances, fearing that such a strategy could weaken NATO's ability to deter Russia from further aggression. But these policy disagreements may not have equal effects on the U.S. interest in a capable and unified NATO. Eastern European allies are highly dependent on the U.S. security guarantee and are unlikely to undermine NATO, even if those allies disagree with U.S. policy. Germany and France, by contrast, could take steps to reduce investments in collective defense in response to disagreements over postwar strategy.

Contents

Figures, Tables, and Boxes

Figures

Tables

Boxes

CHAPTER 1

Introduction

As the fighting in Ukraine continues, contemplating how the United States will deal with Russia after the war is a fraught and challenging endeavor. However, it is crucial to begin thinking through postwar strategy even during wartime. In the past, deep and lasting changes to global or regional order have resulted from decisions made in the immediate aftermath of conflict. The end to this war might come with little warning, and decisions about postwar policies will then have to be made quickly. Therefore, it is important to start these deliberations before the conflict ends so that policymakers have time to weigh the trade-offs of different strategic options. Just as importantly, thinking about U.S. interests in the postwar world could affect U.S. policy toward the war itself.

To inform policymaking about postwar U.S. strategy, we ask:

- What strategic choices will Washington face in determining its approach toward Moscow after the Russia-Ukraine war ends?
- What are the trade-offs associated with those choices?
- To what extent do these trade-offs depend on the war's outcome?

To answer these questions, we conducted an alternative futures analysis, examining the possible effects of different U.S. strategies in different postwar settings. Such an analysis is not intended to predict how events will unfold. Rather, considering alternative futures can help policymakers and the public systematically examine how wartime and postwar choices could interact to affect long-term U.S. interests.

The Importance of Planning for the Postwar Period

Since the full-scale Russian invasion of Ukraine began in February 2022, the United States has—understandably, given the gravity of the situation—been in a mode of continual crisis response. U.S. leaders have worked to build and sustain a coalition to sanction Russia and create an international architecture that can support Ukraine as battlefield conditions change while avoiding a wider or more violent war. Outrage at Russia's flagrant violations of international law and wartime atrocities sustains the U.S. commitment to this set of policies. When the fighting in Ukraine comes to an end, there will be a strong inertial pull to continue many of these wartime policies, a phenomenon political scientists call *path dependency.*

While keeping crisis-response measures in place might be the best approach, it would be a mistake for policymakers not to review and reassess U.S. options. The policy choices that such powerful countries as the United States make—or do not make—in a war's aftermath tend to have long-term effects. Scholars Daniel Deudney and G. John Ikenberry refer to these windows for important decisionmaking after great power wars as *ordering moments,* explaining that

> at these rare junctures, the great powers are forced to grapple with and come to agreement on the general principles and arrangements of international order. These ordering moments not only ratify the outcome of the war, they also lay out common understandings, rules and expectations, and procedures for conflict resolution.[1]

Many of the international institutions that the United States promoted between 1944 and 1951 (during and in the aftermath of World War II), such as the North Atlantic Treaty Organization (NATO), the United Nations, and the International Monetary Fund, remain central to international relations more than 75 years later.[2] The Treaty of Versailles did not just end

---

[1] Daniel Deudney and G. John Ikenberry, "The Unravelling of the Cold War Settlement," *Survival,* Vol. 51, No. 6, December 2009–January 2010.

[2] G. John Ikenberry, *After Victory: Institutions, Strategic Restraint, and the Rebuilding of Order after Major Wars,* Princeton University Press, 2001.

World War I; it also had far-reaching consequences for Germany's domestic politics and relations among European powers.

While the Russia-Ukraine war is not (as of this writing in late 2023) a systemic conflict akin to the world wars and thus might not present a global ordering moment, the endings of smaller-scale wars also have produced agreements that established the contours of regional security architectures and shaped long-term relations among belligerents and their allies. For example, the 1953 Korean Armistice Agreement and the U.S.–South Korea bilateral security treaty (signed soon after the Armistice) have defined the security dynamic on the Korean Peninsula for the past 70 years.

In short, U.S. postwar policy toward Russia could have significant long-term effects on U.S. interests in Europe and beyond. Washington may ultimately decide to keep many elements of its wartime policy, such as elevated force levels in Europe and sanctions on Russia. But whatever postwar policy it adopts, Washington should use the end of the war as an opportunity to make deliberate choices that reflect long-term U.S. goals and the trade-offs associated with different ways of pursuing those goals. Because we do not know when that moment will come, policymakers in the United States should, even as the fighting continues, deliberately weigh its postwar options and consider the long-term effect of wartime decisions.

Overview of Methodological Approach

The world that leaders face after a war often diverges significantly from their expectations.[3] Alternative futures analysis is one way to help policymakers examine their assumptions and explore options and trade-offs when much remains unknown about what comes next.[4] In this report, we provide such an analysis in the context of the Russia-Ukraine war.

---

[3] Alexandra T. Evans, *Alternative Futures Following a Great Power War*, Vol. 2: *Supporting Material on Historical Great Power Wars*, RAND Corporation, RR-A591-2, 2023.

[4] For a more detailed discussion of alternative futures analysis as a method, see Miranda Priebe, Bryan Frederick, Anika Binnendijk, Alexandra T. Evans, Karl P. Mueller, Cortez A. Cooper III, James Benkowski, Asha Clark, and Stephanie Anne Pillion,

Because the Russia-Ukraine war is ongoing as of this writing in late 2023, its outcome is uncertain. Moreover, there are a variety of policies the United States could adopt toward Russia after the war. To simplify this complex problem, we propose a framework to capture the most important aspects of the war's outcome and aftermath. We then apply this framework to generate two different *postwar worlds* (Chapter 2). Chapter 3 describes different overall approaches to U.S. relations with rivals and proposes a framework for generating postwar U.S. policy options toward Russia. We use these constructs to develop two ideal-type postwar U.S. Russia strategies. By interacting the two strategies with the two worlds in which these strategies could be employed, we describe four alternative futures (Chapter 4). For each of the four, we draw on the international relations literature and the history of U.S.-Russia relations to create a narrative about key dynamics in the decade after the war. In Chapter 5, we evaluate how these dynamics would affect U.S. interests. In Chapter 6, we offer observations and conclusions from this alternative futures analysis.

Alternative Futures Following a Great Power War, Vol. 1, *Scenarios, Findings, and Recommendations*, RAND Corporation, RR-A591-1, 2023.

CHAPTER 2

Anticipating the Postwar World

U.S. policy toward a major rival is never conceived or carried out in a vacuum. Therefore, it is essential to take into account the nature of the world in which U.S. postwar strategy toward Russia will be implemented. The contours of that world will be defined by the outcome of the war and the character of the broader international environment. In this chapter, we propose key elements of that postwar setting. We then apply that framework to generate two ideal-type worlds that the United States could face.

Approach to Generating Postwar Worlds

The Russia-Ukraine war is ongoing as of this writing in late 2023. Its trajectory and ultimate outcome are uncertain; many end states are plausible. We focus on those features of the outcome of the war that will have the most significant impacts on the postwar environment. These are six: whether the conflict escalated to a Russia-NATO war (horizontal escalation), whether nuclear weapons were used (vertical escalation), the extent of China's support for Russia during the war, the war's duration and intensity, territorial control (i.e., how much, if any, Ukrainian territory Russia occupies at the end of the war), and the form of conflict termination.[1]

---

[1] We explain the importance of five of these dimensions of the war's trajectory in our prior publication, *Avoiding a Long War*. Here, we add China's support to Russia as a distinct aspect of the war (Samuel Charap and Miranda Priebe, *Avoiding a Long War: U.S. Policy and the Trajectory of the Russia-Ukraine Conflict*, RAND Corporation, PE-A2510-1, 2023).

Even by focusing on this small number of features of the war's outcome, there are myriad variations of each and many ways in which those variations could be combined.[2] To simplify, we developed two ideal-type outcomes: a *less favorable war outcome* that assumes modestly negative variations of the aforementioned features and a *more favorable war outcome* that assumes modestly more positive variations of the features. (We judge favorability from the U.S. perspective.) This means we do not consider extreme war outcomes. For example, we consider some shift in territorial control in favor of one or the other side rather than a Russian occupation of the entire country or a complete liberation of all Ukrainian territory. Because either form of escalation (horizontal or vertical) would be much more than modestly negative, we exclude them from both scenarios. Escalation is, of course, possible, but if it did occur, it would radically redefine the war outcome.[3]

Table 2.1 summarizes the two ideal-type war outcomes, which we describe in more detail in the rest of the chapter.

While the outcome of the war will be a central factor in shaping the context for implementation of U.S. Russia strategy, the broader international environment will be relevant as well. Therefore, we also developed two ideal-type versions of the postwar international environment, which we refer to as the *strategic setting*, that correspond with either the less favorable or more favorable war outcomes. We chose nine key dimensions of the international environment that will define the context in which U.S. policy toward Russia will be implemented, from the state of NATO unity to Russia's relative power.

---

[2] We considered the possibility that some war outcomes might be closely connected to one another and therefore would be highly likely to co-occur. For example, we asked whether a long war is more likely to be accompanied by a weak or robust ceasefire. However, we were not able to find strong evidence in the literature on interstate conflict that the different outcomes would be linked.

[3] Charap and Priebe, 2023; Bryan Frederick, Samuel Charap, Scott Boston, Stephen J. Flanagan, Michael J. Mazarr, Jennifer D. P. Moroney, and Karl P. Mueller, *Pathways to Russian Escalation Against NATO from the Ukraine War*, RAND Corporation, PE-A1971-1, 2022; Bryan Frederick, Mark Cozad, and Alexandra Stark, *Escalation in the War in Ukraine: Lessons Learned and Risks for the Future*, RAND Corporation, RR-A2807-1, 2023.

TABLE 2.1
Two Ideal-Type Russia-Ukraine War Outcomes

Key Aspects of the War	Less Favorable War Outcome	More Favorable War Outcome
Duration	Long war of attrition	Near-term end to the conflict
China's support to Russia	China provided Russia significant amounts of munitions and weapon systems	China continued providing Russia only with nonkinetic capabilities
Form of war termination	Weak ceasefire	Robust ceasefire
Territorial control	Ukraine suffered modest territorial setbacks	Ukraine made modest territorial gains
Escalation to NATO-Russia war	No	No
Nuclear use	No	No

As was the case with the dimensions of the war outcome, we avoided the extremes in the two postwar strategic settings. To keep to two worlds, we linked the two variations in the strategic setting to the two war outcomes. In some cases, there is a tight connection between aspects of the war outcome and dimensions of the postwar strategic setting (e.g., Ukraine's economy will very likely be weaker following a longer war than a shorter war). In other cases, multiple outcomes are plausible and we do not have a strong empirical or theoretical basis to privilege one over the others. In these cases, we defer to more-pessimistic assumptions after the less favorable war and more-optimistic assumptions after the more favorable war. Table 2.2 summarizes the two strategic settings.

We recognize that we have simplified what will be a much more complex picture: In reality, it is unlikely that all nine dimensions will vary in the same way after the war. We also exclude from consideration strategic shocks, such as regime change in Russia, or major events unrelated to the war, such as a conflict in the Indo-Pacific region, that could affect key aspects of the postwar world. Furthermore, our nine dimensions include phenomena, such as U.S. power relative to China, which will be a function of a variety of factors (and the Russia-Ukraine war might not be the most significant of those factors). To facilitate our analysis, we hold all other fac-

TABLE 2.2

Two Ideal-Type Postwar Strategic Settings

Key Dimensions	After the Less Favorable War	After the More Favorable War
Russia's motives	Primarily imperialist, also security-motivated	Primarily security-motivated
Russia's postwar relative power	Russia militarizes its economy and gets help from China so its military power recovers. Still, Russia is not as strong as it was before the war.	Russia's conventional military capabilities are severely weakened by the war. In addition to combat losses, export controls bite, and China does not backfill.
Russia's relationship with China	Security cooperation and trust deepen as a result of China's support during the war.	Russia is irritated over limited support from China. China is irritated about the risks Russia ran during the war (e.g., nuclear threats). Yet both still see their partnership as necessary to counter the United States.
Ukraine's motives	Focused on territorial reconquest	Focused on economic recovery and European integration
Ukraine's economy	Devastated by the long war	Significantly harmed by the shorter war
Transatlantic unity	NATO allies disagreed about whether and how to push for peace as the conflict dragged on. Divisions about postwar policy toward Russia and Ukraine also emerged as the war was ending.	Although allies did not agree on everything, NATO allies remained broadly unified on their orientation toward the war and ceasefire negotiations during the shorter war.
U.S. power relative to China	Russia's relative strength makes it harder to divert U.S. resources to the Indo-Pacific region. China's support to Russia is less draining than U.S. support to Ukraine. Thus, the United States is somewhat weaker relative to China.	There is little impact on the regional distribution of power between the United States and China.
U.S. relationship with China	Relations are worsened by China's provision of lethal weapons to Russia and subsequent U.S. sanctions on Chinese individuals and firms.	The war does not significantly affect U.S.-China relations.

Table 2.2—Continued

Key Dimensions	After the Less Favorable War	After the More Favorable War
Economic relations among rivals	Wartime sanctions on and countersanctions by Russia mean that Russia is less economically integrated with the West than before the war. Western sanctions on China mean that China, to a lesser degree, is beginning to decouple from the West.	Wartime sanctions on and countersanctions by Russia mean that Russia is less economically integrated with the West than before the war. Limited sanctions relief as part of the ceasefire process leaves open the possibility that this trend could reverse.

tors constant by projecting forward the state of the world as of this writing, varying only the outcome of the war. The intent of this alternative futures approach is to provide distinct theoretical (and still plausible) futures that can inform strategic thinking, not to make predictions.

The next section describes the two postwar worlds in greater detail, as defined by the variations in the outcome of the war and the postwar strategic setting in Tables 2.1 and 2.2.

World A: After the Less Favorable War

In this world, developments have transpired that the United States and its allies would have hoped to avoid.

War Outcomes

The fighting settles into a long war of attrition that continues for at least a few more years. During this time, China decides to provide Russia with lethal military support it has hitherto avoided providing, including significant quantities of munitions and advanced weapon systems. With these additional capabilities and more time to address issues plaguing its force, the Russian military makes some territorial gains within Ukraine, taking control of more—but not all—of the five regions it claims to have annexed. In response to Beijing's aid to Moscow, the United States and its allies impose limited sanctions on China, targeting the firms involved in the assistance effort. When the Russian military's offensive appears to have definitively culminated and the Ukrainian military is unable to effectively counterattack, the lines harden into what appears to be a stalemate. Kyiv and Moscow begin talks and eventually reach what we refer to as a *weak ceasefire*, an agreement to end the fighting without sophisticated mechanisms to reduce the risk of conflict recurrence.[4] This leaves the belligerents with a cessation of hostilities more akin to the never-implemented Minsk Agreements than a ceasefire with such measures as a demilitarized zone or a process for addressing violations that are associated with a more durable peace.[5]

Strategic Setting in the Immediate Aftermath of the War

Russia's motives. Russia's motive for its full-scale invasion of Ukraine remains the subject of debate. Some scholars argue that Moscow was driven by imperialistic instincts, while others point to security concerns relating to Ukraine's increasing alignment with the West as the dominant factor.[6] In all likelihood, both motives were at work.[7] We cannot be certain what the balance of these motives will be at the end the war.[8]

---

[4] Unfortunately, there is no standard terminology in international law or in the political science literature to describe the different types of agreements to cease hostilities. On legal usages, see U.S. Department of Defense, Office of the General Counsel, *Department of Defense Law of War Manual*, updated 2016, pp. 864–865.

[5] For evidence about the relationship between more-sophisticated ceasefire measures and lasting peace, see Virginia Page Fortna, "Scraps of Paper? Agreements and the Durability of Peace," *International Organization*, Vol. 57, No. 2, Spring 2003.

[6] For an argument that Russia was entirely motivated by imperialist or expansionist rather than security concerns when invading Ukraine in 2014 and 2022, see Fiona Hill and Angela Stent, "The World Putin Wants: How Distortions About the Past Feed Delusions About the Future," *Foreign Affairs*, Vol. 101, No. 5, September–October 2022.

[7] For the view that states always have mixed security and nonsecurity motives, see James D. Fearon, "Two States, Two Types, Two Actions," *Security Studies*, Vol. 20, No. 3, 2011.

[8] We can make plausible competing arguments about Russia's motives following a war that unfolds as described previously. For example, a longer war could strengthen Russia's imperialist motivations. Even in the first year of the war, imperialist hawks were already ascendant in Moscow, and many elites opposed to the invasion had either left the country or gone silent. School history textbooks are being rewritten to reflect the new imperialist consensus taking hold. These tendencies in Russian society and within elite circles could harden during a longer war. Or, by contrast, a long war without a

Given our more pessimistic assumptions in this world, we assume that imperialist motives dominate. Specifically, we assume that Moscow would view an independent Ukraine as an artificial construct—one that Russia must undo despite the tremendous costs already paid. The idea that Kyiv, the "mother of all Russian cities," would be the seat of power of a deeply anti-Russian government would be intolerable to this Russia. Similar attitudes would be on display toward other former Soviet states, although to varying degrees. While these drivers would push Russia to take actions that go far beyond mere security maximization, Moscow in this world would *also* be driven by traditional security concerns.[9] In other words, while seeking to subjugate Ukraine, Russia would still pursue policies aimed at preserving security, e.g., maintaining a secure second strike capability.[10] We consider a highly imperialistic Russia worse from the U.S. perspective because it will be more prone to aggression toward its neighbors even in the absence of security threats.

Russia's relative power. Russia will likely be weaker relative to NATO and less prosperous than before the war as a result of combat losses and continued sanctions under most plausible war trajectories.[11] Still, the way the war unfolds—especially the length of the war and the nature of China's support—could lead to some variation in just how weak Russia becomes.

---

decisive victory could lead to instability at home, war fatigue, a weakened military, and discrediting of imperialist adventures.

[9] For a discussion of Russian security concerns before the war, see Samuel Charap and Timothy J. Colton, *Everyone Loses: The Ukraine Crisis and the Ruinous Contest for Post-Soviet Eurasia*, Routledge, 2017; Samuel Charap, Dara Massicot, Miranda Priebe, Alyssa Demus, Clint Reach, Mark Stalczynski, Eugeniu Han, and Lynn E. Davis, *Russian Grand Strategy: Rhetoric and Reality*, RAND Corporation, RR-4238-A, 2021.

[10] *Second strike capability* is the ability to retaliate with nuclear weapons if the United States launches a first strike aimed at disarming Russia

[11] On the economic effects of the war to date, see Organisation for Economic Co-operation and Development (OECD), *Economic Outlook, Interim Report*, March 1, 2023; European Council, "Infographic—Impact of Sanctions on the Russian Economy," last reviewed October 12, 2023; Richard Disney, "What Is the Current State of the Russian Economy Under Sanctions?" Economics Observatory, April 27, 2023; and Guy Faulconbridge, "Blood and Billions: The Cost of Russia's War in Ukraine," Reuters, August 23, 2023.

Multiple countervailing trends could affect Russia's relative power by the end of the less favorable war outcome. On the one hand, a longer war would increase Russia's combat losses and could sap military morale and deplete stockpiles. On the other hand, China's decision to provide lethal aid would help to offset Russia's combat losses and backfill high-tech components that had previously been imported from the West. We assume that Moscow could reinvigorate its military-industrial complex during the longer war. Moreover, we assume here that Russia continues to mobilize personnel over the course of the long war and corrects some of the training and leadership deficiencies seen earlier in the conflict.

Consistent with our pessimistic assumptions in World A, this second set of dynamics prevails. Russia is stronger than in World B, though still weaker than before the war.

Russia's relationship with China. In the immediate aftermath of the less favorable war outcome, Moscow and Beijing would most likely be poised to continue deepening their security ties.[12] Russia, having gained greater confidence in its relationship with China during the war, would likely be more open to sharing its own advanced military technologies and engaging in joint weapon system development. Additionally, over time, China might either subtly coerce or induce Russia to change its policies on security issues in the Indo-Pacific region. As the relationship with China becomes ever more important, it is plausible that Moscow might more explicitly support Beijing's positions on regional issues and territorial disputes. Furthermore, China could push for Russia to end sales of high-end military capabilities to Beijing's regional rivals, particularly Vietnam and India, two of Moscow's top military-industrial clients. Beijing could also extract even more favorable energy arrangements from Moscow.

Ukraine's motives. As with Russia, Ukraine's motives at the end of a less favorable war are uncertain. The longer war and territorial losses could have a radicalizing impact. Indeed, we have already seen this dynamic play out in the first two years of the war as a deep hostility toward Russia and an equally deeply held commitment to recover lost territory have progressively

---

[12] Bonny Lin, "The China-Russia Axis Takes Shape," *Foreign Policy*, September 11, 2023.

become more pronounced in both public opinion and government policy.[13] It is plausible that this progression will continue over the course of a longer war. However, it is also possible that a longer war and territorial setbacks could sap Ukraine's military and economy, increase war fatigue, and lead Ukrainians to prefer peaceful development over further fighting.

For this world, we adopt the more pessimistic assumptions (from the U.S. perspective) about Ukraine's motives. We assume that there is a strong popular demand within Ukraine for retaking lost territory and imposing costs on Russia. Ukraine rearms not only to defend the areas it controls but also to eventually oust Russian occupiers from the rest of the country. Although reconstruction and economic development are not neglected as national goals, the government's focus is first and foremost on territorial reconquest and avenging Russia's war crimes, occupation, and brutality. We see this outcome as worse from the U.S. perspective because it means that Ukraine is more likely to resume fighting, regardless of Russia's behavior.

Ukraine's economy. In World A, a longer war has sapped Ukraine's economy. Russia attacked civilian infrastructure, and agricultural areas became battlefields.[14] After several years of fighting, millions of Ukrainian refugees made permanent homes in other countries, shrinking Ukraine's tax base and exacerbating its already significant demographic challenges. Many enterprises closed for good during the longer war. Russia's strikes on infrastructure in major cities sent investors fleeing even from places far away from the line of contact (LoC). The government in Kyiv likely is dependent on external financial assistance for economic survival, and rebuilding would be extremely costly after a long war.[15] In short, the protracted war likely dramatically undermined the country's economic potential. As a

---

[13] Democratic Initiatives Foundation, *Analytical Report Based on the Results of War, Peace, Victory, and Future Survey,* August 16, 2023.

[14] For a discussion of damage to Ukraine's economy in the first year of the war, see World Bank, *Ukraine Rapid Damage and Needs Assessment: February 2022–February 2023,* 2023, p. 10; Joe Janzen and Carl Zulauf, "The Russia-Ukraine War and Changes in Ukraine Corn and Wheat Supply: Impacts on Global Agricultural Markets," *Farmdoc Daily,* Vol. 13, No. 34, February 2023.

[15] World Bank, 2023.

result, in this world, Kyiv likely remains reliant on Western support not only for rearming, but also for fiscal solvency.

Transatlantic unity. Transatlantic unity on support to Ukraine was extremely high early in the war. Even as of this writing, that unity has somewhat slackened: The former Polish government instrumentalized Ukrainian grain imports to attempt to secure reelection, and a party that ran on a platform of ending aid to Ukraine won a plurality in Slovakia's parliamentary election. We assume that, in this less favorable postwar world, these cracks deepen. In particular, as the costs of sanctions mounted, the political will to enforce them weakened, and some allies looked the other way as more-sophisticated evasion techniques undermined their effectiveness. Some allies become less generous in supporting Ukraine as slow growth in the European Union (EU) created trade-offs in spending priorities. The millions of Ukrainian refugees in the EU are highly unlikely to return home, given the economic situation there. Supporting those refugees at the levels offered in 2022 and 2023 might prove to be a financial burden—and a political problem—for host countries, particularly given low labor market participation rates in such countries as Germany, which offered refugees the same social benefits as its own citizens. More disagreements emerged over the types of weapons provided to Ukraine. Allies also disagreed about whether to urge Ukraine to negotiate an end to the war. These divisions appear likely to continue after the war as allies develop different plans for strategy toward Russia and differ in their willingness to support Ukraine. (The divisions envisioned here relate to policy toward the Russia-Ukraine war; we assume that commitment to collective defense of NATO member-states remains strong.)

U.S. power relative to China. The distribution of power in the Indo-Pacific will be driven by many factors, not just the outcome of the war. For simplicity, we assume that there are no major changes in those other dimensions (e.g., a dramatic increase in U.S. defense spending, a crisis in Asia), and instead, we focus only on the ripple of effects of the war.

Multiple countervailing dynamics would affect U.S. power relative to China's in this world. First, the United States focused more on producing new munitions for a land war in Europe while the fighting in Ukraine continued. This included support to Ukraine and allies in Europe as well as for U.S. forces. Beijing's support to Moscow meant that Russia's military strength rebounded somewhat, so the United States continued to worry about Russia's next move. Given industrial base constraints, that means fewer resources were devoted to munitions relevant to Asia contingencies. Additionally, Washington continued to draw down stockpiles of munitions relevant to both theaters for the duration of the protracted conflict. And, in this world, China provided some arms and munitions to Russia, reducing its own stockpiles.

Consistent with our pessimistic assumptions in this world, we assume that Beijing's support to Moscow had less of an impact on Chinese readiness than U.S. support to Ukraine did on American readiness for a conflict in Asia. Moreover, although the United States increased capacity for munitions production during the war, this increase was limited. Therefore, the long and intense Russia-Ukraine war still created real trade-offs for the United States, limiting its power in the Indo-Pacific region.[16] In short, we assume that the net effect of these dynamics is to modestly reduce U.S. power relative to China's. Although this difference does not produce a fundamental shift in the distribution of power in the Indo-Pacific, it is not wholly inconsequential.

U.S. relationship with China. Future relations between Washington and Beijing are not likely to be primarily determined by the Russia-Ukraine war. Still, their policies toward the war will likely have some effect on U.S.-China ties. In this world, we assume that relations worsened over the course of the war, particularly as Beijing began providing lethal aid to Moscow. The United States responded with limited sanctions on Chinese defense firms

---

[16] The demand for munitions in Europe has already led to such a trade-off. For example, weapon deliveries to Taiwan, already delayed as a result of pandemic disruptions, remain behind schedule. In 2023, the United States allowed Taiwan to purchase munitions from U.S. stockpiles rather than, as usual, spending on additional munitions from U.S. manufacturers. The administration has sought to prioritize Asia in future budgets, but in World A, we imagine that the high intensity of the Ukraine war and the time it took to ramp up the industrial base means there was still a trade-off (Tara Copp, "How Ukraine War Has Shaped US Planning for a China Conflict," Associated Press, February 16, 2023; Bryant Harris, "Document Reveals $14 Billion Backlog of US Defense Transfers to Taiwan," *Defense News*, April 14, 2022; Nomaan Merchant, Ellen Knickmeyer, Zeke Miller, and Tara Copp, "US Announces $345 Million Military Aid Package for Taiwan," Associated Press, July 29, 2023; Ashley Roque, "To Combat China, Pentagon Eyeing Multi-Year Munition Buys in FY24," *Breaking Defense*, March 13, 2023).

and became even more committed to a competitive orientation toward the rising power and its increasingly close de facto ally.

Economic relations among rivals. We assume that, in this world, key changes in supply chains, trade patterns, investments, and financial arrangements that began early in the conflict become entrenched.[17] We also assume the following in this world: When China began providing Russia with military aid, U.S. European allies, who had previously sought to stay out of the U.S.-China trade war, joined the United States in imposing limited sanctions on China. In response, Russia and China accelerated development of alternative, non-Western trade and finance mechanisms and relationships during the long conflict. By the end of the war, both countries were more motivated than ever to make themselves less economically dependent on the West. U.S. gross domestic product (GDP) suffered only modestly, but the effects were worse for Europe, leading to a drag on growth and reducing the allies' ability to spend on defense and support Ukraine's rearming and reconstruction.[18]

World B: After the More Favorable War

In this world, we assume a more favorable war outcome and a more benign international environment from a U.S. perspective.

War Outcomes

China sustained its policy of providing nonlethal support to the Russian military but declined to go further. Moscow faced an ammunition shortage

---

[17] For examples of some changes in trade patterns during the war, see Lazaro Gamio and Ana Swanson, "How Russia Pays for War," *New York Times*, October 30, 2022.

[18] For a brief overview of economic effects of the war in Europe and the United States, see Kenneth Rogoff, "The Long-Lasting Economic Shock of War," International Monetary Fund, March 2023; and Elsa Leromain and Marcus Biermann, "How Has the Russian Invasion of Ukraine Affected Global Financial Markets?" Economics Observatory, May 25, 2023. For concerns about a recession in Europe during the war, see Jonathan Cable, "Worsening Euro Zone Business Downturn Reignites Recession Fears," Reuters, July 24, 2023; and Peggy Hollinger, "Russia's War on Ukraine Holds Still More Pain for European Business," *Financial Times*, August 9, 2023.

for its artillery as a result, as well as continued problems with mobilization, morale, and command and control. Russia's military never regained the initiative, and Ukraine retook more of its territory, although it did not retake all that was lost since February 2022. While Ukraine made gains, it did so at a high cost and its forces were exhausted.

We assume that this course of events on the battlefield made Russia and Ukraine more open to negotiations. The United States and many allies also provided incentives (see the following paragraphs) that helped to bring Kyiv and Moscow to the negotiating table before the end of 2024. Russia and Ukraine concluded what we refer to as a *robust ceasefire*, an agreement to stop fighting that includes provisions, such as a demilitarized zone between their forces and a dispute resolution process, to reduce the risk of conflict recurrence.[19]

This outcome became possible because of a parallel set of side deals addressing issues beyond the mechanics of the ceasefire. The United States and the EU offered Russia a path to partial, conditional sanctions relief. *Snapback clauses* in the agreement, similar to those in the Iran nuclear deal, mean that if Russia violates the ceasefire, Western countries will reimpose the sanctions. Many Western countries also formalized commitments to Ukraine that consist of robust economic and military support, including additional aid if Russia invades again—similar to the framework outlined in the July 2023 Group of 7 (G-7) communique.[20] The United States and its allies did not go so far as to provide Ukraine a *security guarantee* (a promise to fight to defend Ukraine against future aggression). But the commitments were nonetheless a powerful incentive to accept the ceasefire. Ukraine and Russia agreed to unilateral political commitments, contingent on the cease-

---

[19] For evidence on the relationship between robust ceasefires and peace, see Virginia Page Fortna, *Peace Time: Cease-Fire Agreements and the Durability of Peace*, Princeton University Press, 2004a. For a proposal for a robust ceasefire in Ukraine, see Samuel Charap, "An Unwinnable War: Washington Needs an Endgame in Ukraine," *Foreign Affairs*, Vol. 102, No. 4, July–August 2023. For comparisons with the Korean armistice, see Carter Malkasian, "The Korea Model: Why an Armistice Offers the Best Hope for Peace in Ukraine," *Foreign Affairs*, Vol. 102, No. 4, July–August 2023; and Andreas Kluth, "Ukraine's Future Isn't German or Israeli but Korean," Bloomberg, August 30, 2023.

[20] Council of Europe, "G7 Joint Declaration of Support for Ukraine," July 12, 2023.

fire holding: Kyiv committed to remain nonaligned, meaning that it will not become a NATO member-state.[21] Russia, in turn, accepted that Ukraine will pursue EU membership and that several NATO allies, including the United States, will provide major economic and military support to enable Ukraine to rearm and rebuild. This quid pro quo was what convinced Moscow to negotiate a robust ceasefire that might serve as an enduring end to the war instead of as an operational pause between phases of fighting.

Neither side gave up its territorial claims—Ukraine insisted on its internationally recognized borders and Russia continued to claim that five Ukrainian regions were its sovereign territory—but they agreed not to continue contesting those claims by force and they established a process to continue negotiations on mutual grievances.

Some might not view this as better outcome from a U.S. perspective because of Ukraine's embrace of nonalignment and thus its forgoing (at least temporarily) the possibility of NATO membership. However, we assume such a concession was necessary to achieve a lasting ceasefire.[22]

Strategic Setting in the Immediate Aftermath of the War

Russia's motives. In this world, we assume that Russia is a primarily security-motivated actor. Therefore, whatever the drivers of its past behavior might have been, in the aftermath of the war Moscow's imperialist urges take a backseat to defending the territory—both disputed and undisputed (i.e., Russia proper)—it does control. Rather than ruminating about the fate of Russian speakers in Ukraine and the need for Eastern Slavic unity, the Russian leadership's priorities are getting its flagging economy back on track and slowly rebuilding its military capabilities. Russia's focus in Ukraine becomes keeping the country out of NATO and NATO forces out of the country. Russia could still resort to force out of security concerns, but in this world, it is less likely to wage war just to realize imperialist ambitions.

---

[21] Ukraine considered such an arrangement as part of peace negotiations early in the war. For a more detailed discussion of security commitments and neutrality as possible elements of a ceasefire or settlement, see Charap and Priebe, 2023.

[22] For a more detailed discussion of why such a concession may be needed, see Charap and Priebe, 2023.

Russia's relative power. In both worlds, Russia is weaker relative to NATO than before the war. Here, we assume that Russia is even worse off than in World A. This may seem counterintuitive because the war in this world was shorter and presumably would lead to fewer Russian combat losses. However, in this world, we make a number of more optimistic (from a U.S. perspective) assumptions about the course of the war that explain why Russia is less able to recover despite this lower level of losses. In World B, we assume that China did not provide lethal aid during the war and Russia's defense industry was less effective in replacing equipment, munitions, and supplies. We also assume here that Russia was less effective at mobilizing and training personnel to offset its casualties.

Russia's relationship with China. In both worlds, Russia-China relations are deeper than before the war. Both countries see the United States as their primary threat and view cooperation with each other as key to mitigating that threat. But, in this world, relations are less close than in World A. Beijing feels that Moscow was reckless (e.g., making nuclear threats) and incompetent (poor military performance). China still sees Russia as a useful partner, but is more worried about getting entangled in the Kremlin's future adventures. Russia remains frustrated by China's refusal to provide lethal military aid during the war. This lower level of trust means that they are not, for example, cooperating on the most sensitive military technologies.

Ukraine's motives. In this world, the Ukrainian leadership's top priorities are economic recovery and European integration. While Kyiv controls more territory than in World A, it became clear by the end of the war that further advances would be extremely costly. In this context, the voices in Ukraine favoring a focus on reconstruction, democracy, EU integration, and economic development in the near term over militarization and territorial reconquest win out—both within the bureaucracy and in election outcomes. Hawks in Kyiv argue that Ukraine should pursue NATO membership and mobilize all its resources to rebuild its military with the aim of retaking its lost territory. However, after a conflict that did serious damage to the economy and killed tens of thousands and with a robust ceasefire in place, these hawks are marginalized. Because of its relatively successful showing on the battlefield and its enhanced security cooperation with Western partners, Ukraine is more confident about its security than in World A.

The robust ceasefire agreement also reduces Ukrainian worries about an imminent resumption of violence.

In this world, Ukrainians come to see reunification as a long-term goal that will be achieved politically when international conditions change. Some in Ukraine note that the collapse of the Soviet Union created an opening for reunification of Germany. So, they reason, domestic unrest and fractures in the Russian state could create an opening for Ukraine's reunification down the road as well. Less dramatically, others hope that a future Russian leader may be more open to territorial negotiations than President Vladimir Putin. In either case, Ukraine intends to make sure that reunification remains appealing to those in Russian-occupied areas through the power of attraction. To do that—and to attract refugees home and rebuild the war-torn economy—the overriding Ukrainian policy priority becomes transforming the country into a prosperous European democracy. Therefore, Kyiv focuses on economic development and the long, arduous task of EU integration.

In addition, the Ukrainian Armed Forces (UAF) leadership recognizes that the robust ceasefire makes any effort to openly contest Russia's control of occupied territory quite risky: Such an attempt would undermine Ukraine's Western support, and the UAF would face difficulty pushing back Russian forces because they were forced to withdraw offensive capabilities back from the LoC as part of the deal. Although Ukraine is not resigned to permanently accepting its territorial losses, liberation fades as a short-term political imperative and becomes a longer-term objective. Of course, Ukraine maintains a substantially more capable military than before the war, but economic recovery is the top priority.

Ukraine's economy. The war has already exacted a significant toll on the Ukrainian economy. GDP fell by a third in 2022, and we can expect grim numbers in 2023 and 2024. Compared with the status quo antebellum, in this world, the country is much poorer and its growth prospects are stunted. But compared with World A, the Ukrainian economy is in far better shape. The extent of the economic damage was much more limited because of the shorter war: More refugees returned, fewer businesses permanently closed, and less infrastructure was destroyed. With adequate reconstruction assistance and EU integration, in this world the Ukrainian economy has a good chance at recovery over time.

Transatlantic unity. In this world, the United States and its European allies remained largely united throughout the war and were buoyed by their contributions to Ukraine's relatively successful performance in the fight. That success and the greater focus on defense and deterrence as a result of Russia's aggression created a strong sense of cohesion and purpose on both policy toward Ukraine and collective defense.

U.S. power relative to China. Because the conflict did not last as long as it did in World A, there was less impact on U.S. power in Asia.

U.S. relationship with China. The war did not have a significant impact on U.S.-China relations. The U.S.-China relationship remains as deeply competitive as it was before 2022.

Economic relations among rivals. In both worlds, Russia is far less integrated into the global economy than before the war. But Russia is marginally more integrated in this world than in World A. The West provided some sanctions relief during the ceasefire negotiations. Nonetheless, Western companies remain reluctant to trade with Russia. The shorter war left some potential for restoration of at least a limited Cold War–style trading relationship between Russia and the West. The extent of global economic fragmentation in this world is less severe because the economic relationship between the West and China was largely unchanged by the war.

CHAPTER 3

Options for Postwar U.S. Strategy Toward Russia

In this chapter, we describe broad U.S. options for approaches to relations with major power rivals. We then propose a framework for developing options for U.S. strategy toward Russia in the postwar context. Finally, we generate two ideal-type U.S. strategies for our futures analysis.

The Spectrum of Approaches to Relations with U.S. Rivals

Options for policies toward a major power rival can be conceived of as falling on a spectrum between, on the one extreme, a very uncompromising approach, such as rollback or even preventive war, and, on the other, a very accommodating approach involving unilateral concessions on key conflicts of interest with the rival. Because neither extreme on this scale represents a plausible U.S. approach toward Russia, it is useful to frame the choice about postwar policy between *hardline* and *less hardline* strategies that are closer to the middle of the spectrum but still distinct. There are divergent rationales for each strategy, as we detail in this chapter.

Hardline Approaches

When a state adopts a *hardline approach*, it seeks to achieve its objectives by outmaneuvering, punishing, or weakening a rival.[1] A state may adopt a

---

[1] Miranda Priebe, Bryan Frederick, Alexandra T. Evans, Samuel Charap, Gabrielle Tarini, and Bryan Rooney, *Future U.S. Peacetime Policy Toward Russia: Exploring the*

hardline approach if it is competing over a vital interest on which it is unwilling to compromise. Even over lesser interests or where compromise appears possible, a state may still choose a hardline approach if it subscribes to the *deterrence model.* According to this logic, a rival with revisionist intentions sees concessions as an indication of weak will. Therefore, compromise, even on less important issues, emboldens the rival to make more demands or to become more aggressive. The Munich analogy is at the heart of this logic: The concessions that British and French leaders made to Adolf Hitler at the Munich conference in 1938, in this view, led Hitler to see the countries as irresolute, emboldening him to undertake further aggression. Rather than reducing tensions, the deterrence model suggests that compromise with a rival only invites further conflict. Conversely, a hardline approach will show resolve and deter further aggression.[2]

Less Hardline Approaches

A *less hardline approach* entails a state pursuing its objectives by addressing some of its rival's interests and concerns. Such strategies are not necessarily cooperative or conciliatory on every policy dimension, nor do they require political rapprochement. However, a less hardline approach does involve some level of compromise through negotiations or unilateral gestures to resolve conflicts of interest.[3]

There are multiple reasons why states choose less hardline approaches. Major powers that face multiple rivals, as the United States does at the time of this writing, sometimes choose to adopt a less hardline approach toward one rival to preserve resources for managing a greater threat. For example, the need to free up resources to respond to challenges posed by China's rise might induce the United States to, at some point, consider a less hardline approach toward Russia. At other times, powers have decided that their objectives vis-à-vis a rival are best served by lowering risks and seeking a degree of common ground for other reasons. For example, the Nixon

---

Benefits and Costs of a Less-Hardline Approach, RAND Corporation, 2023.

[2]   Robert Jervis, *Perception and Misperception in International Politics*, Princeton University Press, 1976.

[3]   Priebe, Frederick, Evans, et al., 2023.

administration pursued détente with the Soviet Union to reduce the risk of conflict and stem the growing costs of the Cold War competition.[4]

Just as the deterrence model is one logic supporting hardline policies, the *spiral model* is a perspective that sometimes motivates calls for a less hardline approach. This model sees security concerns as a root cause of competition and conflict. When a state is insecure, it often adopts such policies as further arming or even aggression to try to increase its security. An action-reaction cycle can, in turn, ratchet up tensions between rivals. In this model, a less hardline approach can reduce some of these security concerns either by resolving a conflict of interest or by communicating more benign intent. By reducing insecurity, the spiral model suggests, a less hardline approach can reduce the risk of future conflict.[5]

Proponents of a less hardline approach are skeptical that compromise emboldens rivals as the deterrence model predicts. They also reject the Munich analogy, noting that not all countries are as ambitious or as powerful as Nazi Germany. Even if a rival were to see the United States as irresolute for adopting a less hardline approach, it is unlikely to have the motive and capability to undertake large-scale opportunistic war.

Framework for Postwar Strategy Toward Russia

Assessing the effects of a given U.S. strategy begins by considering the policies that the United States would pursue under that strategy. We focus here on those policy areas that are likely to be most central in shaping U.S.-Russia relations in the postwar period: strategic stability, U.S. military presence in Europe, the U.S. security relationship with Ukraine, U.S. policy toward other non-NATO former Soviet states, and economic relations with Russia.

Strategic stability has been at the core of relations between Moscow and Washington since the dawn of the nuclear age, and it will certainly remain so going forward. Equally, U.S. military presence in Europe has been central to security dynamics with the Soviet Union and then Russia since the end of World War II. In the period following the conclusion of the Russia-

---

[4] Priebe, Frederick, Evans, et al., 2023.

[5] For a discussion of the spiral model, see Jervis, 1976.

Ukraine war, this aspect of U.S. policy will be more central to overall strategy than before Russia's full-scale invasion of Ukraine because U.S. force numbers on the continent have increased since then. U.S. security assistance to Ukraine and policy toward Russia's other neighbors have been key drivers of tensions in the bilateral relationship since the 1990s.[6] Finally, economic relations with Moscow—or rather what to do about the unprecedented economic sanctions regime that the United States and its allies have imposed on Russia since February 2022—is another question that Washington will have to answer in the aftermath of the war.

Determining U.S. policy in these five issue areas represents a framework for postwar Russia strategy. It is designed to be specific to that future moment; if this exercise were undertaken at a different time, other issues might have displaced some on this list. For example, in 2012, Syria would likely have been on this list, and in 2017, election interference would certainly have been as well.

Applying the Framework

We use the two general approaches toward relations with rivals described previously (hardline and less hardline) to generate the stance that the United States would adopt on these five key issues (see Table 3.1). For the purposes of our analysis, we developed ideal types of postwar strategy: a hardline approach that entails taking a tougher line across all dimensions of U.S. policy toward Russia, and a less hardline approach that involves adopting a somewhat more accommodating stance on all these dimensions. In reality, the United States could pursue less hardline policies on some issues and more hardline policies on others. But framing the choice as binary allows for a better understanding of the implications of a strategic-level decision to pursue one approach or the other.

---

[6] Charap and Colton, 2017.

TABLE 3.1

Two Ideal-Type Postwar Strategies Toward Russia

Aspects of U.S. Policy	Hardline Approach	Less Hardline Approach
Strategic stability	• Unwillingness to engage in strategic arms control negotiations • Competitive new nuclear capability development and force posture • Deployment of more BMD installations in Europe and Asia • Deployment of intermediate-range ground-based missiles in Europe	• Willingness to pursue strategic arms control negotiations • Restraint on nuclear weapon policy • Willingness to adopt de facto or agreed limits on U.S. ballistic missile defense (BMD) • Open to a moratorium or cap on intermediate-range ground-based missiles in Europe
Military presence in Europe	• Sustainment of elevated wartime force levels in Europe • Deployment of more of these forces into Eastern Europe • Rejection of talks on limiting U.S. and allied deployments in NATO countries	• Drawing down of forces from wartime peak • No additional forces deployed to Eastern Europe • Willingness to engage in talks on limitations on force levels or locations
Security relationship with Ukraine	• Provision of funds, arms, and training, with a focus on enabling offensive maneuver • Steps toward integrating Ukraine's military with NATO, including increased interoperability • Stated support for NATO's open door and eventual Ukrainian membership	• Provision of funds, arms, and training optimized for a defensive posture • No major attempts to integrate Ukraine's military into NATO or increase interoperability • Openness to Ukraine's neutrality and no promotion of Ukraine's membership in NATO
Policy toward other non-NATO former Soviet states	• Support for Georgia's integration into the alliance and rhetorical support for membership • Stepped-up security cooperation activities with non-NATO former Soviet states • Systematic effort to rollback Russian influence	• No further steps toward NATO integration or membership for Georgia • Reduction in security cooperation levels with non-NATO former Soviet states compared with wartime • Only limited efforts to undermine Russian influence on its periphery
Economic relations with Russia	• Sustainment of most wartime sanctions on Russia	• Willingness to negotiate further conditional sanctions relief

Hardline Approach

Strategic Stability

Strategic stability in U.S.-Russia relations encompasses both (1) the disposition, numbers, and posture of U.S. strategic capabilities and (2) Washington's willingness to engage with Moscow in discussions on limiting or restraining those capabilities. The United States makes decisions about these issues on the basis of the size of not just Russia's arsenal, but also China's (and North Korea's). Therefore, we need to make some assumptions about overall U.S. policy on nuclear weapons and related capabilities that go beyond strategy toward Russia.

For the hardline approach, we assume that the United States adopts a strategy of nuclear superiority in the postwar period. This policy includes "expansive offensive counterforce capabilities, offensive and defense damage limitation capabilities, and flexible and tailored limited nuclear options to deter adversaries at any level of conflict."[7] Washington seeks a force posture that could, in a crisis, allow the United States to launch a strike that would destroy large numbers of Russian and Chinese nuclear forces simultaneously, with the aim of limiting damage from any retaliatory attack. Given China's nuclear buildup, this would entail increasing the number of warheads the United States could deliver, by uploading existing intercontinental ballistic missiles (ICBMs) and submarine-launched ballistic missiles so that they each carry more warheads, and increasing the planned purchase of next-generation ICBMs, ballistic missile submarines (SSBNs), and heavy bombers. Although these modernized systems might not come online during the postwar decade, the projected future force would have an impact on Russian and Chinese decisionmaking long before that.

This approach would entail a more significant investment in BMD systems, traditionally seen by Moscow as potentially capable of blunting Russia's ability to launch a retaliatory second strike. The United States could install additional systems in Europe that are capable of intercepting Russian missiles, such as Aegis Ashore Mk-41 vertical launchers with SM-3 mis-

---

[7] David Kearn, Jr., *Reassessing U.S. Nuclear Strategy*, Cambria Press, 2019, p. 92.

sile interceptors.[8] The United States could increase the frequency of Aegis-capable surface ship patrols, which carry the same missile interceptors, in the Baltic and Black Seas.

In Europe, the United States would field new ground-based missile systems that were banned under the now-defunct Intermediate-Range Nuclear Forces (INF) treaty. For example, the Army would deploy its Long-Range Hypersonic Weapon, with a range of 2,700 kilometers, to Germany,[9] and the Army's Strategic Mid-Range Fires, a shorter-range cruise-missile, to Poland.[10] Although both systems are conventionally armed, Russia has traditionally seen European deployments of missiles with this range as posing the threat of a prompt strike against Russia's nuclear command, control, and communications systems.[11]

The hardline strategy would embrace the end of legally binding U.S.-Russia arms control. Advocates of this policy would question the point of bilateral arrangements in an era of Chinese buildups, which, these advocates argue, undermines the case for any limitations on the U.S. arsenal. Furthermore, they point to Russian suspension of the New START Treaty (NST) during the Russia-Ukraine war as clear evidence that Moscow cannot be trusted to comply with any agreements. "No more arms control with Russia" becomes official U.S. policy.

---

[8] As of this writing in late 2023, one Aegis Ashore (in Romania) is operational and another is set to go online imminently (Andrew Eversden, "Missile Defense Chief 'Confident' Poland's Aegis Ashore Ready in 2023," *Breaking Defense*, August 12, 2022).

[9] Andrew Feickert, *The U.S. Army's Long-Range Hypersonic Weapon (LRHW)*, Congressional Research Service, IF11991, updated September 15, 2023a.

[10] Andrew Feickert, *The U.S. Army's Strategic Mid-Range Fires (SMRF) System (Formerly Mid-Range Capabilities [MRC] System)*, Congressional Research Service, IF12135, November 28, 2023b.

[11] For example, fears of such decapitation strikes were among the key drivers of the Euromissile crisis that began in 1977 and ended with the 1987 INF treaty (Gordon Barrass, "Able Archer 83: What Were the Soviets Thinking?" *Survival*, Vol. 58, No. 6, December 2016–January 2017).

U.S. Military Presence in Europe

In response to Russia's aggression in Ukraine, the United States increased its force presence in Europe to around 100,000 military personnel by deploying or extending the deployments of about 20,000 U.S. personnel.[12] U.S. forces also moved east. The United States deployed attack aviation from Germany to Lithuania; Patriot theater air defense systems from Germany to Slovakia and Poland; and F-15 tactical fighters from the United Kingdom to Poland. Washington characterized these changes as part of a wartime surge to deter Russia from expanding its aggression beyond Ukraine to attacks on U.S. allies.

The hardline approach would keep U.S. forces at these levels and locations despite the war's end. The United States would also work bilaterally with allies in Eastern Europe to enable additional U.S. deployments or prepositioning of equipment in countries east of Germany. Washington would point to the increased unpredictability and uncertainty created by Russian aggression and the need to reassure skittish allies. Although the enhanced deterrence need was created by the Russia-Ukraine war, it did not diminish in the war's aftermath, U.S. officials would argue.

In addition, the United States and its allies would be unwilling to engage Russia in a follow-on agreement to the now-defunct Treaty on Conventional Armed Forces in Europe (CFE). Washington would not be willing to discuss mutual reductions in its conventional forces on the continent or limitations on where such forces could be deployed. Moreover, pointing to Russia's past noncompliance with conventional arms control mechanisms, Washington would argue that there is even less reason to believe that Moscow would comply with any constraints, given its norm-busting behavior during the war.

Security Relations with Ukraine

The hardline approach would extend the extraordinary wartime U.S. security assistance to Ukraine in the postwar period. Through July 2023, the United States had provided $43 billion in military aid. Building on the G-7 security

---

[12] U.S. Department of Defense, "Fact Sheet—U.S. Defense Contributions to Europe," June 29, 2022c.

commitments to Ukraine signed at the Vilnius NATO summit in July 2023, the United States would provide the UAF with extensive ongoing assistance.[13]

During the war, U.S. support was channeled toward helping Ukraine develop a force capable of defending areas that it already controls and mounting offensive operations to retake lost territory. We refer to this as an *offensive maneuver–capable* force. If it adopts the hardline strategy, the United States would continue this policy after the war.

The United States would also push to admit Ukraine into NATO in the immediate aftermath of the war and, barring that, seek to cement an extremely close relationship and keep the door open for possible future membership. This effort would include joint exercises (outside Ukraine), assistance to promote interoperability between Ukrainian and NATO forces, and regular political consultations in the NATO-Ukraine Council. The U.S. objective would be for Ukraine to be in the position of Finland before it made the decision to join the alliance in 2022—so deeply integrated that formal membership would be a de jure codification of what would be, for all intents and purposes, a de facto reality. Rhetorically, the United States would reiterate its support for NATO's open-door policy on a regular basis and with specific reference to Ukraine, underscoring continued U.S. adherence to the pledges made in the 2008 Bucharest and 2023 Vilnius summits that Ukraine "will become" a member and that its "future is in NATO."[14]

Relations with Other Non-NATO Former-Soviet States

The hardline approach would entail the United States undertaking efforts to roll back Moscow's influence in the other non-NATO states that are located between the alliance and Russia, particularly Moldova and Georgia, but also nominal Russian allies Armenia and Belarus and farther-afield Central Asian states. Essentially, countering Russia becomes the top U.S. priority in relations with these countries, leading to a deprioritizing of democracy and human rights. Practically, that would entail support for upgrading Georgia's integration with NATO by giving it the same privileges and level of inte-

---

[13] Council of Europe, 2023.

[14] NATO, *North Atlantic Treaty*, signed at Washington, D.C., 1949; NATO, "Bucharest Summit Declaration," April 3, 2008.

gration as Ukraine, such as eliminating the need for a membership action plan and creating a NATO-Georgia Council. Washington would support Belarusian opposition movements and seek to create elite splits in Minsk. Washington would subsidize Moldova's pro-Western government to prevent a possible electoral loss to the pro-Russian opposition. Washington would offer Yerevan greater opportunities for security cooperation, seeking to take advantage of Armenia's disillusionment with Russia's role as patron. In Central Asia, the United States would provide regional states any possible opportunity to demonstrate political distance from Russia. Throughout the region, the U.S. military would be active in training local forces and joint exercises.

Economic Relations

The United States and its allies implemented unprecedented sanctions against Russia following its full-scale invasion of Ukraine in February 2022. These measures included placing export controls on a variety of high-tech goods, freezing Russian Central Bank reserves, choking off much of the Russian banking sector from the global financial system by blocking U.S. dollar transactions, banning Russian airlines from U.S. airspace, revoking permanent normal trade relations, outlawing imports of several key Russian products, seeking to impose a price cap on Moscow's oil exports, and so on. All of this was done in the name of imposing costs for Russia's aggression in Ukraine.

While we posit that selective, conditional sanctions relief might be necessary to reach a ceasefire, the hardline strategy would take an uncompromising line in the postwar period, demanding full withdrawal of Russian forces from all of Ukraine in return for further relief. This means, for example, if Russia and Ukraine engage in negotiations in the postwar period (such as over prisoner swaps), Washington would not be willing to offer sanctions relief to help Kyiv get a better deal. The hardline approach would therefore continue all or most sanctions imposed since February 2022 after the war in Ukraine comes to an end.[15]

---

[15] Arguably, this is the most likely outcome, given that the United States has historically found it much harder to lift than to impose sanctions (Richard Nephew, "The Hard Part: The Art of Sanctions Relief," *Washington Quarterly*, Vol. 41, No. 2, 2018).

Less Hardline Approach

Strategic Stability

With the less hardline approach, the United States would seek to reduce the role of nuclear weapons in U.S. defense policy when possible, consistent with the Biden administration's Nuclear Posture Review.[16] The nuclear modernization program of record would proceed as planned with one-for-one replacements of existing launchers and warheads. However, Washington would not seek to deploy more strategic warheads or launchers than allowed under the NST. Instead, Washington would seek to counter any Chinese or Russian nuclear buildup with existing capabilities or conventional means.

Under this approach, the United States would continue the policy announced by the Biden administration of seeking discussions with Russia on a follow-on agreement to the NST without preconditions.[17] Washington would be willing to agree to limits on those weapon systems that are covered by the NST and to expand bilateral arms control to cover more categories of nuclear weapons, such as nonstrategic nuclear weapons (NSNWs), and an overall limit on warheads.

Under this less hardline approach, the United States would not upgrade its existing BMD architecture and would be open to transparency measures regarding its existing interceptors in Europe. Washington would consider incorporating mutual restraints on BMD into a potential future arms control regime or undertaking unilateral self-restraint commitments regarding future BMD plans, particularly because treaty-based BMD limitations might not be politically viable.

The United States would also be open to negotiations over intermediate-range nuclear forces. In September 2019, Putin proposed a moratorium on the deployment of intermediate-range ground-based missiles after the INF

---

[16] See the Biden administration's *2022 Nuclear Posture Review*, which repeatedly cites the "goal of reducing the role of nuclear weapons in U.S. strategy" (U.S. Department of Defense, *2022 Nuclear Posture Review*, 2022a).

[17] Jake Sullivan, "Remarks by National Security Advisor Jake Sullivan for the Arms Control Association (ACA) Annual Forum," June 2, 2023.

treaty had come to an end.[18] Russia reiterated the offer in October 2020.[19] Reportedly, during 11th-hour negotiations to avert war in January 2022, the United States indicated an openness to discussing the Russian proposal.[20] While bilateral negotiations on this issue have been shelved during the war, a less hardline approach in peacetime would entail Washington once again demonstrating openness to negotiating mutual restraints on ground-based intermediate-range missiles in Europe. By the time the war comes to an end, some U.S. intermediate-range cruise or hypersonic missiles might have already been deployed to Europe, but likely not in large numbers. In that case, a moratorium rather than a regional cap on such missiles might be more plausible.

U.S. Military Presence in Europe

The less hardline approach would reduce U.S. military presence in Europe in the postwar period. As noted, U.S. force numbers in Europe increased by 20,000 during the war, and U.S. forces moved farther east.

In the postwar period, the United States would reduce these forces through negotiations or unilaterally. Before merely pulling back the forces from east to west and from Europe to the continental United States, the less hardline approach would first seek to negotiate mutual restraints on conventional forces in Europe with Russia. The United States would attempt to reach an agreement on geographic constraints on Russian forces deployed near the border with NATO and in Belarus, as well as limits on military activities (such as major exercises) in those areas. The purpose of these talks would be to limit Moscow's ability to launch a surprise attack on frontline allies and provide advance warning of concerning activities. In return, Washington would consider reciprocal pledges to limit its own deployments

---

[18] Elena Chernenko, "Vladimir Putin's Letter Reached the Right Addressee," *Kommersant*, November 27, 2019.

[19] President of Russia, "Statement by Vladimir Putin on Additional Steps to De-Escalate the Situation in Europe in the Context of the Termination of the Intermediate-Range Nuclear Forces (INF) Treaty," October 26, 2020.

[20] Hibai Arbide Aza and Miguel Gonzalez, "US Offered Disarmament Measures to Russia in Exchange for Deescalation of Military Threat in Ukraine," *El País*, February 2, 2022.

east of Germany—or at least not to increase them. But even if such negotiations fail, the less hardline approach would entail an eventual postwar U.S. drawdown of forces on the continent.

Security Relations with Ukraine

Under both strategies, Kyiv would remain a major recipient of U.S. military aid at levels higher than before the war. This would include the long-term security assistance provided under the arrangements concluded as part of the G-7 July 2023 statement of support for Ukraine.[21] This assistance would come in the form of direct provision of military equipment, training of the Ukrainian military at U.S. facilities in Europe and the continental United States, and the regular exchange of intelligence information. However, under the less hardline approach, U.S. security assistance would be focused on helping the Ukrainian military optimize its forces for defense rather than developing an offensive maneuver–capable force.

Such a "porcupine strategy" would aim to defend areas under Ukrainian government control, not enable offensive operations to retake areas occupied by Russian forces.[22] There are many overlaps between the training and materiel that the United States would provide to Ukraine under the two different approaches to military posture. For example, air defense systems and tanks would be useful for both a defense-optimized and an offensive maneuver–capable force. But there would be important differences in emphasis. A porcupine strategy might, for instance, call for the United States to help Ukraine develop a mine-laying capability to make a future Russian offensive more difficult. To support an offensive maneuver–capable posture, the United States might instead help the UAF develop the breaching and mine-clearing capabilities it would need to retake territory that has been heavily mined by Russia. The less hardline approach would limit the provision of certain capabilities to the UAF, such as long-range strike. The United States would instead help Ukraine harden its infrastructure and provide a larger number of survivable defensive systems, such as mobile air defenses and

---

[21] Council of Europe, 2023.

[22] For the logic of the porcupine strategy, see William S. Murray, "Revisiting Taiwan's Defense Strategy," *Naval War College Review*, Vol. 61, No. 3, Summer 2008.

short-range fires. In addition, Washington would make it clear to Kyiv that it would lose U.S. military support if it initiates further hostilities.

The less hardline strategy would entail a restrained U.S. approach to Ukraine's relationship with NATO. The United States would not take radical steps away from existing policy, such as renouncing the open door or the 2008 Bucharest summit declaration. But Washington would not actively promote further discussion of Kyiv's membership prospects. Its security assistance would focus less on transforming the UAF to prepare it for membership (i.e., emphasizing NATO standards and interoperability) and more on helping Ukraine develop the capabilities to defend itself under the porcupine strategy. Although Washington would not formally close the door on Ukraine's eventual membership in the alliance, it would support any move initiated by Kyiv to embrace neutrality (as it did in the March 2022 Istanbul Communique).[23] The U.S. logic would be to avoid signaling that Ukraine is moving toward imminent NATO membership, which could lead to an aggressive Russian response.

Relations with Other Non-NATO Former Soviet States

The less hardline approach would prescribe a restrained policy toward the other non-NATO former Soviet states. For example, Washington would not push for Georgia's closer integration with NATO, even if a pro-NATO government came to power in Tbilisi. Moreover, under the less hardline approach, security cooperation with other non-NATO Russian neighbors would revert to levels consistent with the status quo ante bellum, reversing instances where it has been enhanced since the war.

More broadly, the United States would not prioritize stamping out all vestiges of Russian influence in the region. This approach would be driven by a number of factors: a desire to avoid gratuitously stoking tensions with Moscow, an understanding that Russian influence is at an all-time low as a result of Russia's own actions and that this diminution is likely to continue without any additional U.S. efforts, a recognition that regional economies need access to Russia for growth, and a view that geopolitical competition has undermined stability and set back the prospects for reform in these

---

[23] Farida Rustamova, "Ukraine's 10-Point Plan," *Faridaily* blog, March 29, 2022.

states. Washington would not stand idly by if Russian malign activities were to spike in a given country. But, barring such contingencies, averting regional tensions would be seen as more important than countering Russia at every turn.

Economic Relations

With the less hardline strategy, the United States would consider relieving some sanctions on Russia on a conditional basis. For example, the United States would be willing to offer sanctions relief to help Ukraine gain concessions from Russia in postwar negotiations (e.g., on freedom of movement for Ukrainians in occupied territories or access to power from the Zaporizhzhia nuclear power plant). Given Russia's ongoing occupation and its lack of contrition for its war crimes even in the more favorable war outcome, the United States would not return to status quo ante bellum economic relations under this strategy.

CHAPTER 4

Alternative Postwar Futures

In the previous chapters, we described two postwar worlds—defined by the outcome of the war and the nature of the broader international environment in its aftermath—and two possible U.S. strategies toward Russia. In this chapter, we generate four alternative futures by interacting each strategy with each world. We gave the futures titles that capture the key dynamics in the postwar decade (Table 4.1). These future scenarios focus only on developments related to the outcome of the war and U.S. strategy toward Russia. We do not consider other international dynamics that could emerge in the decade after the war.

We describe each future in the sections that follow, beginning with a description of the motives behind U.S. strategy given the postwar context. We then identify some key dynamics that could emerge in the decade following the war as a result of the United States pursuing that strategy in the given world. We describe these dynamics by drawing on the international relations literature on conflict, rivalry, and alliance dynamics, as well as the history of U.S.-Russia relations. However, this literature suggests possibilities and likelihoods rather than certain outcomes. Therefore, we provide our best assessment of the most likely postwar dynamics in each future, but note that other scenarios might well be plausible given the same starting points.

TABLE 4.1
Alternative Futures in the Decade After the Russia-Ukraine War

	Hardline U.S. Approach	Less Hardline U.S. Approach
World A: after the less favorable war	Future 1: Pervasive instability	Future 2: Localized instability
World B: after the more favorable war	Future 3: Cold War 2.0	Future 4: Cold peace

Future 1: Pervasive Instability

Given the **less favorable war outcome**, the situation in Ukraine is unstable, with both Kyiv and Moscow preparing to resume the conflict as soon as they can recover, regroup, and reequip. To keep Russia weak and deter it from future aggression against Ukraine or NATO allies, the United States adopts a **hardline approach** that entails punishing the Kremlin for its past transgressions while strengthening U.S. allies and partners (see Box 4.1). In the decade following the end of the war, the result is a greater risk of NATO-Russia conflict and a nuclear conflict between the United States and Russia (and to a lesser extent China) than before the war (see Box 4.2 for a summary of these dynamics).

U.S. Motive: Deter Russia Through Strength

While the guns have fallen silent, the United States believes Russia is biding its time, unsatisfied with its territorial gains from the war, and committed to future land grabs. The United States believes that the best way to deter the militarized, aggrieved, and not fully beaten-down Russia is to keep it weak, strengthen Ukraine, and more deeply integrate Kyiv with NATO.

The United States also believes that China is watching U.S. policy closely and that coddling Russia will embolden China. U.S. leaders reason that taking a hard line against Moscow will send a strong signal to Beijing that aggression does not pay.[1]

Key Postwar Dynamics

Ukraine focuses on unconventional operations while it rebuilds its military. Despite substantial U.S. support, a reconquest-focused Ukraine needs time to rearm and rebuild its depleted military before it can contemplate an offensive to retake its territory. In the meantime, Ukraine's leaders feel they must keep contesting Russian control over the country's sovereign territory—despite the ceasefire—so neither Ukrainians nor the country's

---

[1] This logic of signaling resolve to other potential aggressors has been at work in U.S. policy during the war (Cindy Saine, "Biden Cites US Resolve in Facing Aggression from Russia and China," Voice of America, February 8, 2023).

BOX 4.1

Future 1: Postwar World and U.S. Strategy

World A: After the Less Favorable War	Hardline Approach
War outcomes	**Strategic stability**
• The conflict ends after a long war of attrition	• Reject arms control negotiations
• China provides lethal aid to Russia	• Develop new nuclear capability and expand force posture
• The war ends in a weak ceasefire	• Deploy more BMD installations
• Ukraine suffers modest territorial setbacks	• Deploy intermediate-range ground-based missiles to Europe
Strategic setting in the immediate aftermath of the war	**Military presence in Europe**
• Russia is primarily imperialist, also security-motivated	• Sustain elevated force levels
• Russia is weakened by the war, but poised to rearm	• Deploy more forces into Eastern Europe
• Russia-China relations are very close	• Is not open to talks on limiting deployments in NATO countries
• Ukraine is focused on territorial reconquest	**Security relationship with Ukraine**
• Ukraine is economically devastated	• Provide assistance that enables offensive operations
• NATO is divided over wartime policy toward Russia and Ukraine	• Integrate Ukraine's military with NATO
• U.S. shift to the Indo-Pacific region is limited by the war in Europe	• Support open door and Ukrainian membership
• U.S.-China tensions exist because of Beijing's support for Moscow	**Policy toward other non-NATO former Soviet states**
• There is global economic fragmentation because of sanctions and counter-sanctions	• Support Georgia's NATO integration and membership
	• Increase security cooperation with regional states
	• Roll back Russian influence
	Economic relations with Russia
	• Sustain most wartime sanctions

partners begin to treat the occupation as permanent. Kyiv's near-term focus is therefore on unconventional operations, including support to insurgent groups in the Russian-occupied territories. The United States looks the other way as Kyiv engages in these ceasefire violations.

With U.S. help, Ukraine continues developing its offensive combined-arms capability. Kyiv seeks the capacity to push through the LoC and over-

BOX 4.2
Key Dynamics in Future 1: Pervasive Instability

- Ukraine focuses on unconventional operations while it rebuilds its military.
- With U.S. help, Ukraine continues developing its offensive combined-arms capability.
- Some allies' military support to Ukraine declines.
- Ukraine moves toward NATO, but full membership remains elusive.
- Ukraine's economy does not recover, and its democracy erodes.
- Some allies' economic support to Ukraine wanes, and Kyiv's hopes for EU membership dim.
- Russia continues its imperialist agenda in the postwar decade.
- Competitive dynamics in post-Soviet Eurasia increase.
- NATO is initially divided over U.S. force posture enhancements.
- Russia counters U.S. force posture enhancements in Europe.
- A Russia-China de facto alliance forms.
- A new U.S.-Russia arms race heats up.
- NATO allies eventually circle the wagons as allies see Russian behavior as increasingly threatening.
- NATO defense spending plateaus.
- China accelerates its nuclear modernization and buildup, fueling the arms race.
- The global economy moves toward blocs.

run Russian forces in key locations to liberate territory. U.S. willingness to provide high-end offensive weapon systems along with relevant training and enablers helps the UAF move toward becoming a modern force capable of combined-arms offensives.

Some allies' military support to Ukraine declines. The long war depleted European stockpiles and drained the coffers of even the wealthiest NATO member-states. Some European capitals also worry that further war is more likely because of Ukraine's ceasefire violations and "offensively motivated" rearming. These allies are reluctant to provide weapons and military aid to promote what they see as a reckless Ukrainian strategy.

Ukraine moves toward NATO, but full membership remains elusive.
The United States, the United Kingdom, Poland, and some other Eastern
European allies call for Ukraine to be granted NATO membership on the
West German model, meaning even before it has resolved its territorial disputes.[2] However, Germany, France, Hungary, and others block the move.
Under pressure from the United States, they agree to sustain rhetorical support for Ukraine's eventual membership. They also support greater Ukrainian integration with NATO short of full membership, such as enhanced
exercises, training, and interoperability with NATO forces.

Kyiv incrementally inches toward NATO membership as the United
States helps the UAF become more interoperable with NATO forces and
continues to rhetorically support the open-door policy. Although the lack
of consensus among allies means that Ukraine does not receive a formal
invitation to join the alliance during the decade following the war, the U.S.
expectation is that, over time, Ukraine will become so asymptotically close
to joining that the final step will eventually seem a mere formality.

**Ukraine's economy does not make a major recovery, and its democ-
racy erodes.** With this emphasis on rearming and territorial reconquest
over stability, reconstruction, and reform, Ukraine struggles to revive its
war-shattered economy. The United States provides economic aid, but these
funds are channeled toward building a war economy, which is not necessarily optimized for growth. The strong possibility of another war limits
private investment. Moreover, refugees do not return in significant numbers
because of the lack of jobs and degraded social services awaiting them in
Ukraine, and instead they make permanent homes in their host countries.
Ongoing militarization goes hand in hand with continuation of emergency
measures and the extreme centralization of power, leading to the erosion of
democratic institutions, checks and balances, and the rule of law.[3]

**Some allies' economic support to Ukraine wanes, and Kyiv's hopes
for EU membership dim.** Some allies reduced their financial support to

---

[2] For a discussion of the West German model, see François Heisbourg, "How to End a
War: Some Historical Lessons for Ukraine," *Survival*, Vol. 65, No. 4, August–September
2023.

[3] For a discussion of this dynamic historically, see Anna Lührmann and Bryan Rooney,
"Autocratization by Decree: States of Emergency and Democratic Decline," *Comparative Politics*, Vol. 53, No. 4, July 2021.

Ukraine and enforcement of sanctions on Russia during the long war.[4] In the postwar period, the EU proves less generous in its aid to Ukraine than was expected. Member-states are less willing to continue wartime levels of direct budgetary support because of the trade-offs with domestic spending. Moreover, the growing sense among European governments is that Ukraine is both reckless and no longer converging toward EU standards of governance, which limits their willingness to help rebuild Ukraine's infrastructure and economy. Nor will the EU put a militarized and increasingly autocratic Ukraine on an accelerated membership track. The United States continues to provide aid, but Washington cannot fully make up for the loss of European support. In a vicious cycle, Ukraine's weak economic recovery, partially driven by instability, further dims its prospects of eventual EU membership. This outcome is driven largely by the duration of the war, the weak ceasefire, and Ukraine's postwar focus on liberating territory by force. Moreover, the hardline U.S. policy that enables Ukraine's militarization exacerbates European discomfort with support to Ukraine and the country's trajectory.

Russia continues its imperialist agenda in the postwar decade. Russian forces repress civilians and crack down violently on Ukraine's allies (both imagined and real) in the occupied areas. Moscow also orders cross-border and cross-front raids to disrupt Kyiv's sabotage efforts. In other words, Russia, like Ukraine, violates the terms of the ceasefire. The situation on the ground becomes increasingly volatile, and the LoC skirmishes appear to be powder kegs. Russia also undertakes intensive information operations in Ukraine to degrade popular support for the government in Kyiv. Moscow seeks to cultivate new allies using bribery and offers of renewed access to the Russian market. Moscow takes advantage of increasing divides within Ukrainian society to advance its interests and undermine Kyiv's deepening ties with NATO.

Still driven by an aggressive imperialist drive to conquer more of Ukraine—a motive fueled further by security concerns relating to U.S.

---

[4] For a prediction that this could happen as the war continues, see Ivan Krastev and Mark Leonard, "Peace Versus Justice: The Coming European Split over the War in Ukraine," ECFR Policy Brief, No. 452, June 15, 2022.

military assistance to the country and Kyiv's deepening ties with NATO—Russia rebuilds to resume the war.

Competitive dynamics in post-Soviet Eurasia increase. The United States steps up security cooperation, assistance, and political engagement with other non-NATO former Soviet states besides Ukraine, particularly Moldova, Georgia, Armenia, and even (to a lesser extent) Belarus. Across the board, engagement with all these countries trumps concerns about enabling autocracy. Increased U.S. security cooperation with Georgia and its not-so-subtle support to the pro-Western opposition leads Russia to worry that the United States is going to push for Georgia to move toward NATO membership. Moldova becomes a flashpoint as a result of its domestic divide between pro-Russian and pro-Western parties, which provides easy avenues for Russia and the West to take sides. The imperialist attitude prevailing in Moscow drives a hyperactive Russian policy across the region, not only to keep the West out but also to subjugate the region's states to the Kremlin's diktat. U.S. hardline policies and Russian imperialism are a toxic mix, leading to backsliding on reform as local elites appeal to external patrons for support.

NATO is initially divided over U.S. force posture enhancements. With enthusiastic support from some NATO allies in Eastern Europe, such as Poland, the United States moves more forces, including ground-launched cruise missiles, into Eastern Europe. These posture changes provoke divisions within the alliance. Because there is no NATO consensus on Washington's plan to have more-substantial permanent deployments east of Germany—specifically, to eastern Poland, Latvia, and Finland—the United States works bilaterally with these countries to make it happen, as it did in 2007 when it reached agreements to deploy components of its BMD system to Poland and Czechia with the host governments directly. France and Germany withdraw the forces that had been deployed in Eastern Europe, citing the lower threat from Russia following the end of the war. Their opposition does not stop the United States from proceeding with its posture enhancements.

Russia counters U.S. force posture enhancements in Europe. With China's support, Russia rebuilds its military after the war ends. In response to the U.S. buildup in Europe and increasing political tensions with the United States, Russia follows through on its 2022 plans to recreate the Leningrad Military District and deploys two new divisions to the Western Military

District.[5] Russia establishes a formal base in and deploys forces to Belarus to counter NATO deployments in Poland. Tensions are exacerbated by Russian snap exercises conducted in the areas bordering Finland or the Baltic states every time NATO forces begin joint exercises there.

Russian military strategists and senior officers' writings suggest that they anticipate a conflict with NATO would begin with an aerospace attack and involve many high-end capabilities that had not been used in the Ukraine war.[6] Therefore, Moscow spends more on integrated air defense, C4ISR (command, control, communications, computers, intelligence, surveillance, and reconnaissance), advanced submarines, anti-satellite systems, longer-range missiles, and next-generation tactical aviation.

A Russia-China de facto alliance forms. Russia-China ties, already strengthened through military cooperation during the war, deepen politically, militarily, and economically after the war. Continued U.S. sanctions on Chinese firms involved in that cooperation, combined with the hardline approach toward Russia, drive the two countries closer together than ever. They increase technology transfers and joint efforts on new military capabilities to counter U.S. advantages. This cooperation expands into technologies related to strategic capabilities as a nuclear arms race heats up.

A new U.S.-Russia arms race heats up. More than 50 years of U.S.-Soviet and U.S.-Russian efforts to limit their nuclear arsenals and ensure strategic stability are definitively over. Citing Russia's wartime announcement that it would suspend implementation of the NST, the United States withdrew less than a year before the treaty was due to expire in 2026. Although it was unwilling to return to the treaty, Moscow wants to restart strategic stability talks to lay the groundwork for a new agreement, but the United States is not interested. This leaves no bilateral treaties or even engagements on strategic stability issues at a time of high political tension. Beyond the limits in the treaty, the notifications, data exchange, and inspections that the NST established have not been operational since the Russian suspension in 2023. As

---

[5] "Russia's Defense Chief Proposes Re-Establishing Moscow, Leningrad Military Districts," TASS, December 21, 2022.

[6] Sergei Chekinov and Sergei Bogdanov, "The Essence and Content of the Evolving Notion of War in the 21st Century," *Military Thought*, Vol. 1, 2017.

the years pass, mutual uncertainty about the status of the two states' nuclear arsenals grows as intelligence gaps emerge.

Beyond arms control, Washington is adopting policies that, from Moscow's perspective, undermine strategic stability. Before the war, Moscow had already been concerned about its ability to maintain a secure second strike capability. Long-planned modernized U.S. delivery systems, such as the Sentinel ICBMs and *Columbia*-class SSBNs, are ordered in larger numbers than originally planned, further increasing Moscow's concern about the survivability of Russia's main deterrent forces. These insecurities grow as the United States expands BMD and deploys intermediate-range missiles in Europe after the end of the war. Moscow feels increasingly vulnerable to a disarming strike in a crisis or nuclear blackmail and unfettered U.S. coercion in peacetime.

To maintain its assured retaliation capability, Russia begins uploading additional warheads onto its existing delivery systems, exceeding the NST limits of 1,550 deployed strategic nuclear warheads. Russia doubles down on its so-called exotic nuclear weapons, which all are focused on ensuring retaliation.[7] Russia also engages in nuclear saber-rattling, hoping to force the United States to rethink its stance. For example, Russia starts dazzling U.S. satellites when they observe Russian ICBM fields, activity that had been prohibited under the NST. Russia also moves more NSNWs closer to NATO countries, including into Belarus and Kaliningrad.[8] Moscow televises deployments of several Poseidon nuclear doomsday autonomous drone torpedoes. It also threatens to renew nuclear testing.

The United States responds to Russia's provocative nuclear activities with further buildups of its own. The United States convinces its NATO allies to repeal the 1996 ministerial declaration of the "three nos"—that NATO had

---

[7] Samuel Charap, John J. Drennan, Luke Griffith, Edward Geist, and Brian G. Carlson, *Mitigating Challenges to U.S.-Russia Strategic Stability*, RAND Corporation, RR-A1094-1, 2022; Jill Hruby, *Russia's New Nuclear Weapon Delivery Systems: An Open-Source Technical Review*, Nuclear Threat Initiative, 2019.

[8] Such a move would not be unprecedented. Russia began moving weapons into Belarus in 2023 ("Ukraine War: Putin Confirms First Nuclear Weapons Moved to Belarus," BBC News, June 17, 2023). It is unclear what, if any, nuclear weapons Russia already has in Kaliningrad (Jonathan Masters and Will Merrow, "Nuclear Weapons in Europe: Mapping U.S. and Russian Deployments," Council on Foreign Relations, March 30, 2023).

"no intention, no plan, and no reason" to deploy nuclear weapons on the territory of new member-states.[9] The United States supports Poland joining the NATO nuclear mission and begins helping Poland prepare to host and operate dual-capable aircraft (those that can carry both conventional and nuclear weapons). The United States also begins building secure storage sites in Poland for U.S. nuclear gravity bombs.

NATO allies eventually circle the wagons as allies see Russian behavior as increasingly threatening. Eastern NATO allies support the hardline U.S. approach from the outset. Germany and others initially oppose it as excessively provocative toward Russia. However, over time, even skeptical NATO member-states come to see Russia's behavior as destabilizing. Moscow's nuclear policy, conventional buildup along its borders with NATO countries, and imperialistic behavior along its periphery lead to a shared view that Russia is a dangerous actor that needs to be checked with a united front. Unity therefore strengthens on the core NATO mission of defense and deterrence.

NATO defense spending plateaus. Although allies eventually come to a common view on the threat that Russia poses, the risk of another war in Ukraine and the gradual process of global economic fragmentation (discussed in more detail later in this section) slow economic growth in Europe, straining domestic support for higher levels of defense spending. Allies spend more on defense than they did before the war, but they do not meet the targets they originally envisioned.

China accelerates its nuclear modernization and buildup, fueling the arms race. China historically maintained a relatively small nuclear force. In the years before the war, however, Beijing began expanding its nuclear arsenal. These changes were seemingly driven, at least in part, by concerns that U.S. missile defense and prompt global strike capabilities threatened China's ability to retaliate.[10]

---

[9] NATO, "Final Communiqué," statement at the meeting of the North Atlantic Council Defence Ministers Session, M-NAC(DM)-3(96)172, December 18, 1996.

[10] For an overview of China's historical nuclear posture and factors driving decisions about it, see Fiona S. Cunningham and M. Taylor Fravel, "Assuring Assured Retaliation: China's Nuclear Posture and U.S.-China Strategic Stability," *International Security*, Vol. 40, No. 2, Fall 2015. For a discussion of recent changes in China's nuclear

The U.S. decision to invest in more and better strategic offensive and defensive capabilities affects China's perceptions as well as Russia's. The end of U.S.-Russia arms control agreements further complicates matters: Chinese planners no longer can count on legally binding caps on U.S. nuclear weapons. This creates acute uncertainty in Beijing about its assured retaliation capability, particularly in light of U.S. plans for more modernized ICBMs, heavy bombers, and SSBNs, which could just as easily be employed against China as Russia. In response, China accelerates its modernization program and plans to deploy a larger arsenal. Beijing's actions, in turn, fuel calls in the United States for even more nuclear weapons.

The global economy starts dividing into blocs. By the end of the longer war, Russia is economically isolated from the West. China, while still maintaining deep economic relations with the West, is modestly less integrated because of wartime sanctions. In the postwar period, policy changes on both sides continue the gradual process of decoupling. Moscow and Beijing continue to prioritize reducing their vulnerability to Western sanctions, especially with the prospect of another war and a hardline Washington. China's wartime support to Russia and deepening security cooperation with a state that clearly has unresolved imperialist ambitions in Ukraine make European allies more willing to heed long-standing U.S. warnings about their economic reliance on China. The United States and its allies adopt policies to promote economic ties among themselves (e.g., free trade agreements) and industrial policies to promote greater self-sufficiency. These policy changes are slow and limited because the West does not seek to pay too high an economic price in the process. Still, over the decade, these policies gradually increase global economic fragmentation. India and countries in the Global South continue to work with both emerging blocs. Overall, the process of economic fragmentation that started before the war continues in the postwar period, reducing—though by no means eliminating—economic ties between the rival blocs.[11]

---

posture, see Joby Warrick, "China Is Building More Than 100 New Missile Silos in Its Western Desert, Analysts Say," *Washington Post*, June 30, 2021.

[11] For a discussion of fragmentation in global commodity markets since the start of the war, see International Monetary Fund, *World Economic Outlook: Navigating Global Divergences*, October 1, 2023.

Future 2: Localized Instability

The **less favorable war outcome** prompts a strategic rethink in the United States and a decision to adopt a **less hardline approach** toward Russia (see Box 4.3). U.S. leaders believe that little was gained for U.S. interests from the years of fighting, while the diversion of munitions, weapon systems, and other resources to Ukraine left the United States less prepared for conflict elsewhere. Moreover, by demonstrating the limits of Russia's power and eroding it, the war convinces U.S. leaders that Russia represents a much less significant threat to U.S. interests than had been believed—and certainly a less significant threat than China. The risk of conflict recurrence in Ukraine—as a result of the escalation of dynamics along the line of contact—is still high. But in this future, the risks of a NATO-Russia conflict or nuclear crises are lower than in Future 1 (see Box 4.4 for a summary of these dynamics).

U.S. Motive: Shift the Focus to China

The U.S. mindset in this future is to reduce the risk of another conflict in Europe as a means toward the end of focusing U.S. resources on the Indo-Pacific. The United States was Ukraine's staunchest supporter in the war from 2022 onward, but as the war dragged on, questions grew about whether the U.S. resources and attention devoted to Ukraine were the best ways of promoting U.S. interests.

U.S. leaders do not want to be called on to arm and assist Ukraine through another protracted war. Instead, Washington is eager to focus on the comprehensive challenge posed by China and is mindful of fiscal constraints at home. Washington also hopes to limit the extent of Russia-China security cooperation that came out of the war and make progress on other stalled issues of global governance, such as climate change.

Much as the long wars in Afghanistan and Iraq led to a rethink of the U.S. role in the Middle East and a shift in focus to great power competition, the protracted war in Ukraine leads to a reevaluation of the U.S. role in Europe. Russia does not appear capable of overrunning Ukraine. And even a more militarized Russia is not poised to attack U.S. allies. NATO's deterrent effect was strong even during the hot war. As a result, U.S. leaders see

BOX 4.3

Future 2: Postwar World and U.S. Strategy

World A: After the Less Favorable War	Less Hardline Approach

War outcomes
- The conflict ends after a long war of attrition
- China provides lethal aid to Russia
- The war ends in a weak ceasefire
- Ukraine suffers modest territorial setbacks

Strategic setting in the immediate aftermath of the war
- Russia is primarily imperialist, also security-motivated
- Russia is weakened by the war, but poised to rearm
- Russia-China relations are very close
- Ukraine is focused on territorial reconquest
- Ukraine is economically devastated
- NATO is divided over wartime policy toward Russia and Ukraine
- U.S. shift to the Indo-Pacific region is limited by the war in Europe
- U.S.-China tensions exist because of Beijing's support for Moscow
- There is global economic fragmentation because of sanctions and counter-sanctions

Strategic stability
- Open to arms control negotiations
- Restraint on nuclear weapons policy
- Open to limits on U.S. BMD
- Open to limits on intermediate-range ground-based missiles in Europe

Military presence in Europe
- Draw down forces
- No additional forces to Eastern Europe
- Open to talks on CFE-like limitations

Security relationship with Ukraine
- Provide assistance for a defensive posture and resiliency
- Do not integrate Ukraine's military into NATO
- Open to Ukraine's neutrality no promotion of NATO membership

Policy toward other non-NATO former Soviet states
- No steps toward Georgia's NATO integration or membership
- Reduce security cooperation with regional states
- Limit efforts to undermine Russian influence

Economic relations with Russia
- Open to conditional sanctions relief

BOX 4.4
Key Dynamics in Future 2: Localized Instability

- Without the prospect of U.S.-provided offensive capabilities, Ukraine adopts a porcupine strategy.
- Ukraine's economy does not recover, and its democracy erodes.
- The United States reduces its forces in Europe from the wartime high.
- NATO allies are divided on postwar policy toward Russia.
- Allies provide more military support to Ukraine than in Future 1.
- The United States and Russia make modest progress on nuclear arms control.
- Ukraine contests Russian control of occupied areas.
- Russia also violates the ceasefire.
- Russia rebuilds, focused on pursuing its imperialist ambitions in Ukraine.
- Some allied support for Ukraine wanes.
- Russia-China relations remain strong.
- Russia continues to seek influence in its neighboring states, but with a less heavy hand..
- Global economic divisions do not accelerate.

the risk of a Russia-NATO conflict in the postwar period as low and would like to keep it that way. Moreover, all-out competition with Russia in the countries of non-NATO Europe is not seen as a winning proposition. Therefore, U.S. policymakers attempt to stabilize the competition with Russia and begin to gradually normalize the relationship. Although U.S. leaders hope that this less hardline approach toward Russia will free up resources for other theaters, they are not ready to go as far as some strategists, who call for a full U.S. military withdrawal from Europe and a fundamental change in the U.S. role in NATO.[12] Nor do U.S. leaders expect that their modestly less hardline approach toward Russia can entirely transform the U.S.-Russia relationship.

---

[12] For such a proposal, see Barry R. Posen, *Restraint: A New Foundation for U.S. Grand Strategy*, Cornell University Press, 2014.

Key Postwar Dynamics

Without the prospect of U.S.-provided offensive capabilities, Ukraine adopts a porcupine strategy. As in Future 1, both Kyiv and Moscow are preparing for a second round of conflict. The United States believes that the best way to deter Russia from launching another war is to help Ukraine rearm with a defensive posture, thereby convincing Russia that it would be unable to achieve its goals in Ukraine militarily at a reasonable cost. Washington also hopes to avoid giving Moscow the impression that another war is inevitable; therefore, the United States avoids giving Ukraine arms that might give the Kremlin an incentive to preventively attack. Furthermore, the United States does not want to give Ukraine the capability to pursue its aims of reconquest.

To strike this delicate balance, the United States encourages Ukraine to adopt a porcupine strategy, which means making Ukraine very hard and costly to conquer by ensuring that it has a force optimized for defense, as we detailed in Chapter 3. Washington makes clear that its support to Ukraine is conditional: U.S. aid will stop if Kyiv initiates a war to retake its territory (Box 4.2). Ukraine is still motivated by desires to eject the Russians, but Kyiv sees little other choice in the short term than to accept the type of support the United States provides.

Finally, the United States knows that Russia wants to forestall Ukraine's integration with NATO and may use force once again to prevent it. Given the periodic ceasefire violations on both sides, Washington (with support from Berlin and Paris) makes the case that any invitation for Ukraine to join NATO would be premature.

Ukraine's economy does not make a strong recovery, and its democracy erodes. As in Future 1, Ukraine's emphasis on territorial reconquest over stability, reconstruction, and reform limits its postwar economic recovery. Democratic institutions and the rule of law also suffer as they did in Future 1.

The United States reduces its forces in Europe from the wartime high. The United States starts reducing the number of forces in Europe because major combat operations in Ukraine are over, lowering the risk to allies. The war showed that Russia was highly reluctant to attack NATO, even while allies supported Ukraine and implemented punishing sanctions. Moreover, Russia is weaker than before the war, making a deliberate attack on NATO even less likely. Given these realities, the United States does not believe it needs to sustain the extra forces deployed to Europe in wartime to deter a Russian attack on a NATO country in the postwar period.

Although the United States has expressed its openness to engaging with Russia on a follow-on to the CFE to get something in return for the planned U.S. withdrawal, Moscow's bellicose mood complicates matters. Russian foreign policymakers and the top military brass dismiss out of hand the prospect of NATO member-state inspectors visiting their bases. Talks on conventional arms control do not get very far. But the United States still sees little risk in reducing forces to pre-war levels. After all, Russia's Western Military District forces are a shadow of their former selves, and European allies are all building up their own militaries.

NATO allies are divided on postwar policy toward Russia. Some NATO allies, such as France and Germany, support the less hardline approach to Russia and the restraints on support to Ukraine. Other allies, such as Poland, lobby Washington against the less hardline approach. Ultimately, despite some pressure from the U.S. Congress, the administration in Washington sticks to its course, and the disgruntled allies mostly resign themselves to the new policy. They worry that they could lose U.S. support themselves if they go too far in pushing Washington or taking steps on their own that contradict the U.S. position, such as providing Ukraine with the offensive weapons or training the United States is withholding.[13] As with the abortive move by Warsaw to put MiG-29 fighters "at the disposal of the Government of the United States of America" in the early days of the war rather than giving them directly to the Ukrainians—and its immediate climbdown when Washington refused—Warsaw ultimately is loath to act without American support on arms transfers.[14] As a result, even Ukraine's staunchest defenders place limits on their support to Ukraine.

---

[13] For such alliance abandonment concerns, see Glenn H. Snyder, "The Security Dilemma in Alliance Politics," *World Politics*, Vol. 36, No. 4, July 1984.

[14] U.S. Department of Defense, "Statement by Pentagon Press Secretary John F. Kirby on Security Assistance to Ukraine," March 8, 2022b; Ministry of Foreign Affairs of the Republic of Poland, "Statement of the Minister of Foreign Affairs of the Republic of Poland in Connection with the Statement by the US Secretary of State on Providing Airplanes to Ukraine," August 3, 2022.

Allies provide more military support to Ukraine than in Future 1. Some allies are more willing to provide support to Ukraine's defensively oriented military than they were in Future 1, in which the United States was helping Ukraine build an offensive maneuver–capable force. That said, such allies' support is still limited by their own economic challenges and concerns about Ukraine's ceasefire violations.

The United States and Russia make modest progress on nuclear arms control. Russia is an unappealing (to put it mildly) partner in the postwar period because of all that happened during the war and Moscow's continued lack of contrition for its crimes. Still, driven by the perceived need to avoid a three-way arms race, the United States wants to engage Russia on issues of strategic stability now that the last remaining bilateral arms control agreement, the NST, has expired, after several years of Russian noncompliance with the inspection, notification, and data exchange provisions following its so-called suspension of the treaty in February 2023. Washington seeks to extend the three central limits of the NST—on deployed strategic warheads, launchers, and deployed launchers—that Moscow did observe as unilateral commitments, instead of negotiated treaties. Moscow agrees, but there is little chance of returning to legally binding arms control after the longer war, if only because ratification of a treaty by the U.S. Senate is a nonstarter. Long-standing Russian fears of decapitating strikes from ground-based systems in Europe drive a positive response to a U.S. offer to negotiate a politically binding cap on ground-based INF-range systems on the continent.

Moscow agrees to these limits because it remains concerned about U.S. efforts to gain first-strike advantages, and it sees arms control as one way to mitigate the U.S. threat. During the war, Russia's proximate concerns about events on the ground had led it to try (ineffectively) to use its withdrawal from the NST as a coercive weapon aimed at reducing U.S. support to Ukraine. In the postwar setting, restrictions on U.S. military and political support to Ukraine—precisely what the Kremlin had tried to effectuate during the war—and the less hardline U.S. approach toward Russia more generally make Moscow more willing to treat arms control, once again, as a compartmentalized, protected issue in the relationship.

Ukraine contests Russian control of occupied areas. The United States encourages Ukraine to comply with the spirit and letter of the ceasefire agreement. U.S. leaders hope to re-create the lasting peace that had followed the combat phase of the Korean War. In that case, the U.S. ally, the Republic of Korea (ROK), was exhausted, just as Ukraine is at the end of this war.[15] As in Korea, the United States now makes clear it will not support an offensive campaign by its Ukrainian partner.[16] However, major differences between the Korean armistice and the Ukraine-Russia ceasefire soon become evident: Russia is far less ground down than was the Democratic People's Republic of Korea (DPRK), and there is no outside player to restrain Moscow, as China did for the DPRK.[17] In this context, Washington also finds it is less able to restrain Kyiv. Ukrainian leaders feel that they must respond to Russia's ongoing occupation of Ukrainian territory, relentless repression of Ukrainians who resist, and continued Russian military buildup. Moreover, Kyiv assesses that Washington will find the domestic and international political cost of abandoning Ukraine too high, and thus it can resist American pressure. In short, Washington is unsuccessful at restraining Kyiv's unconventional activities in occupied areas, even though it is Ukraine's biggest supporter.[18]

Because the United States does not help Ukraine develop its offensive maneuver capability as in Future 1, Ukraine has less conventional capacity to contest Russian control of the occupied territory. However, it does not take a lot of resources to undermine Russian authority in the occupied areas, impose costs, and take revenge for the war that just ended. Ukraine uses special forces to conduct cross-boundary raids, sabotage military and civilian infrastructure in Russian-held areas, and provide insurgents who operate in those areas with supplies and funds.

---

[15] Donald W. Boose, Jr., "The Korean War Truce Talks: A Study in Conflict Termination," *Parameters*, Vol. 30, No. 1, Spring 2000; William Stueck, *The Korean War: An International History*, Princeton University Press, 1995; William Stueck, "Conclusion," in William Stueck, ed., *The Korean War in World History*, University Press of Kentucky, 2004.

[16] Boose, 2000; Stueck, 1995.

[17] For a discussion of outside powers' efforts to restrain the ROK and DPRK, see James I. Matray, "Korea's War at 60: A Survey of the Literature," *Cold War History*, Vol. 11, No. 1, 2011; Stueck, 1995.

[18] U.S. attempts to restrain its allies and partners from using force have not always been successful, especially when it regards an ally's core interests (Jeremy Pressman, *Warring Friends: Alliance Restraint in International Politics*, Cornell University Press, 2008).

Russia also violates the ceasefire. As in Future 1, Russia seeks to "finish the job" in southeastern Ukraine by expanding its territorial control. Russia cracks down violently on Ukraine's allies (both imagined and real) in the occupied areas and conducts its own cross-border and cross-front raids to disrupt Ukraine's sabotage efforts. In other words, Russia, like Ukraine, violates the terms of the ceasefire. As in Future 1, the situation on the ground becomes increasingly volatile.

Russia rebuilds, focused on pursuing its imperialist ambitions in Ukraine. As in Future 1, Russia is rearming expeditiously with China's help. But in this future, Moscow prioritizes capabilities for a second round of fighting in Ukraine. Russia does not beef up its forces on the border with NATO or increase investments in preparations for an aerospace conflict with the alliance because the threat is declining (as a result of the drawdown of U.S. forces in Europe and lower U.S.-Russia tensions).

Some allied support for Ukraine wanes. Wealthy NATO allies initially support Ukraine in line with the defense- and resilience-focused posture, as noted previously. However, these allies' support wanes as it becomes clear that Ukraine is violating the ceasefire. As in Future 1, Ukraine's democratic erosion leads to its EU membership process stalling and EU aid being limited.

Russia-China relations remain strong. The deepening of Russia-China relations that accelerated during the war is largely locked in, and Moscow's intention to further deepen those ties is unshaken by the subsequent U.S. shift in focus away from Europe.[19] Despite the less hardline U.S. approach, the United States still sees and treats Russia as a rival, not a partner. The less hardline U.S. approach turns down the dial on competition and does not push Russia even further into China's arms in the postwar period, but this approach was never intended to transform the U.S.-Russia relationship. In the Kremlin's view, the United States remains the number one threat, and Moscow's postwar ties with Beijing strengthen its ability to respond to that threat. Beyond its security motives to sustain its ties with China, Russia

---

[19] These trends began before the war as both countries increasingly sought to counter U.S. power and influence (Andrew Radin, Andrew Scobell, Elina Treyger, J.D. Williams, Logan Ma, Howard J. Shatz, Sean M. Zeigler, Eugeniu Han, and Clint Reach, *China-Russia Cooperation: Determining Factors, Future Trajectories, Implications for the United States*, RAND Corporation, RR-3067-A, 2021).

sees a lot to gain from its deepened relationship, particularly economic benefits. No one in Moscow is making the case for sacrificing these ties simply because Washington has somewhat reduced its threatening posture.

Russia continues to seek influence in its neighboring states, but with a less heavy hand. As was the case during the war, Russia's imperialist energies are largely focused on Ukraine. Moscow lacks the bandwidth to pursue another military adventure, so it resorts to the usual bullying, bribing, and pressure that has marked its relations with the former Soviet states since 1991. The reduction in U.S. engagement in the region diminishes the geopolitical competition over loyalties compared with Future 1. But that competition is not completely absent.

Global economic divisions do not accelerate. In the postwar period of Future 2, the process of economic fragmentation is not as rapid as in Future 1. The United States does not push its allies as hard to limit ties with China. The United States and its allies also lift some sanctions on Russia in the postwar period. However, Western companies do not rush back to rebuild economic relationships in Russia, so the effect is small. Russia and China continue their efforts to reduce reliance on the West, but not to the same extent as in Future 1 given the lower level of great power competition. Therefore, trends toward fragmentation continue, but at a slower rate than in Future 1.

Future 3: Cold War 2.0

After the **more favorable war**, the United States adopts a triumphalist **hardline approach** toward Russia (see Box 4.5). The dynamics in this future lead to a lower risk of a second war in Ukraine. But Russia-NATO tensions and nuclear risks are elevated, resulting in a second cold war in Europe featuring regional and strategic instability (see Box 4.6 for a summary of these dynamics).

U.S. Motive: Take Advantage of Russia's Weakness

As in Future 1, the United States is motivated to adopt a hardline approach to strengthen Ukraine and deter Russia and other revisionist powers by demonstrating that aggression does not pay. In this future, Washington is

BOX 4.5
Future 3: Postwar World and U.S. Strategy

World B: After the More Favorable War	Hardline Approach
War outcomes	**Strategic stability**
• The war ends soon	• Reject arms control negotiations
• China does not provide Russia with lethal aid	• Develop new nuclear capability and expand force posture
• The war ends in a robust ceasefire	• Deploy more BMD installations
• Ukraine makes modest territorial gains	• Deploy intermediate-range ground-based missiles to Europe
Strategic setting in the immediate aftermath of the war	**Military presence in Europe**
• Russia is primarily security-motivated	• Sustain elevated force levels
• Russia is severely weakened by the war and its defense industry is struggling	• Deploy more forces into Eastern Europe
	• Is not open to talks on limiting deployments in NATO countries
• Russia-China relations are somewhat strained	**Security relationship with Ukraine**
• Ukraine is focused on economic recovery	• Provide assistance that enables offensive operations
• Ukraine's economy is significantly harmed by the war	• Integrate Ukraine's military with NATO
• NATO maintained unity on wartime policy toward Russia and Ukraine	• Support open door and Ukrainian membership
• U.S. shift to the Indo-Pacific region is not significantly limited by the war in Europe	**Policy toward other non-NATO former Soviet states**
• The war does not have a major impact on U.S.-China tensions	• Support Georgia's NATO integration and membership
• Russia is much less economically integrated with the West	• Increase security cooperation with regional states
	• Roll back Russian influence
	Economic relations with Russia
	• Sustain most wartime sanctions

also driven to take advantage of Moscow's weakness to kick a great power rival while it's down, so to speak. The U.S. attitude is that there is little Russia can do to prevent the United States from pursuing its goals, regionally or globally.

BOX 4.6
Key Dynamics in Future 3: Cold War 2.0

- Ukraine remains committed to the ceasefire.
- Ukraine adopts a forward defense posture.
- Allies help rearm Ukraine.
- Ukraine integrates more deeply with NATO while maintaining formal neutrality.
- Allies' economic aid and support for EU membership help to fuel Ukraine's economy.
- The hardline U.S. strategy exacerbates Russia's security concerns, but Ukraine's restraint mitigates them compared with Futures 1 and 2.
- Russia and Ukraine do not make progress on a political settlement.
- Moscow increases gray zone activities in NATO countries in response to anxieties over the U.S. buildup in Eastern Europe.
- Moscow takes steps to counter U.S. moves in non-NATO former Soviet countries.
- A new U.S.-Russia arms race heats up.
- China accelerates its nuclear modernization and buildup, fueling the arms race.
- China and Russia team up against a common strategic foe.
- Divisions persist within NATO over postwar strategy .
- Russia-West economic decoupling gains steam in the postwar period.

Key Postwar Dynamics

Ukraine remains committed to the ceasefire. An economic development–oriented Kyiv is eager to avoid a resumption of hostilities. Therefore, it does not engage in unconventional warfare and uses the consultation mechanisms to address disputes over the ceasefire with Russia rather than turning first to military responses.

Ukraine adopts a forward defense posture. At the end of the war, Ukraine's strategy changes from liberating territory to defending the territory it already controls. The United States does not press Ukraine to adopt a porcupine strategy in this future, and the wartime policy of providing capabilities for offensive maneuver and deep strikes is on autopilot. As a result, Ukraine transitions the UAF to a forward defense posture that is aimed at holding enemy supply lines and bases deep within Russia at risk as a deterrent. For Moscow, this posture is harder to interpret as defensive than the porcupine approach in Future 2 because it could more easily transition to an offensive strategy.

Allies help rearm Ukraine. Ukraine's respect for the ceasefire and emphasis on development over reconquest helps to sustain allies' commitments to helping Ukraine rearm. The EU's better economic performance after the shorter war also makes it easier for allies to find room in their budgets for this support.

Ukraine integrates more deeply with NATO while maintaining formal neutrality. Kyiv continues to see closer relations with NATO as key to deterring Russian aggression against territory it controls. Even though Kyiv adopted neutrality as part of the armistice, Ukraine welcomes U.S. support to help it integrate with NATO. Kyiv goes right up to the limit of technical compliance with the nonalignment pledge but does not violate it.

Allies' economic aid and support for EU membership help to fuel Ukraine's economy. The European economy's relatively better state, given the shorter war, means that all allies have more capacity to contribute than in Futures 1 and 2. As Ukraine focuses on developing its economy and strengthening its democratic institutions, and as war seems less likely to resume over time (see Chapter 5 for details), European countries invest heavily in Ukraine's economy and its integration into the EU. Full membership in the economic alliance is still a long-term prospect, but full integration into the single market is increasingly a reality, and access to EU structural funding for Ukraine proves transformative. As economic growth resumes and the security situation stabilizes, many Ukrainian refugees return home, supporting Ukraine's recovery.

The hardline U.S. strategy exacerbates Russia's security concerns, but Ukraine's restraint mitigates them compared with Futures 1 and 2. Ukraine's integration with NATO and acceptance of U.S. assistance in building an offensive maneuver–capable force leave Moscow on edge despite the stability along the LoC, thanks to the robust ceasefire. But, ultimately, Ukraine's restraint makes these concerns less acute than in Future 1 and 2.

Russia and Ukraine do not make progress on a political settlement. While they continue to implement the armistice and its ceasefire-support mechanisms over the decade, the parties face challenges in translating that achievement into a broader détente. Irreconcilable territorial claims persist. But even more-modest steps prove elusive. Moscow's uncertainty about Kyiv's intentions (with respect to NATO membership and commitment to the ceasefire) and a lack of active U.S. support for talks—there is no diplomatic engagement or willingness to consider concessions on sanctions or other issues to help the parties find a deal—lead to a largely dormant political process.

Moscow increases gray zone activities in NATO countries in response to anxieties over the U.S. force buildup in Eastern Europe. As many hawks in Russia had predicted, agreeing to the ceasefire did not translate into a more conciliatory postwar U.S. policy. U.S. deployments in Eastern Europe heighten Russia's sense of vulnerability. These concerns are even more acute than in Future 1 because of Russia's comparatively weaker conventional military. Lacking the means to respond in kind with its own buildup, Moscow resorts to gray zone activities—e.g., information operations, stepped-up intelligence activities, political interference—in NATO countries to undermine alliance unity.

Moscow takes steps to counter U.S. moves in non-NATO former Soviet countries. As in Future 1, stepped-up U.S. security and economic cooperation with non-NATO states on Russia's periphery and U.S. support to democratic movements accentuates threat perceptions in the Kremlin. In Future 1, however, an imperialistic Russia seeks not only to limit Western influence in the region but also to subordinate its neighbors. In this future, a security-motivated Russia continues to meddle in the affairs of its neighbors to counter U.S. influence, but it does not seek total control. Moreover, Russia's resources are more constrained in this future. But given the limits of U.S. influence in the region, the security threats there are secondary to the U.S. conventional buildup in Europe and the emerging strategic arms race.

A new U.S.-Russia arms race heats up. As in Future 1, hardline U.S. policies—refusal to reengage in arms control, deployments of intermediate range ground-based missiles and more BMD infrastructure in Europe, and the nuclear buildup (uploading of existing missiles and expanded buy of new systems)—stoke Russian concerns about the vulnerability of its assured retaliation capability. These concerns are heightened because of Russia's conventional weakness in this future, but Moscow's responses largely mirror Future 1: Russia engages in a nuclear buildup and nuclear signaling to try to convince the United States to return to arms control negotiations and, failing that, to deter the United States from thinking that it has the capability to launch a splendid first strike on Russia. Additionally, as in Future 1, Russia's rearmament focuses on those capabilities it considers necessary for the NATO fight, such as anti-satellite systems, advanced submarines, and C4ISR.

China accelerates its nuclear modernization and buildup, fueling the arms race. As in Future 1, China's concerns that the United States may be pursuing a more unrestrained nuclear policy lead it to devote even more resources to its own nuclear program. Acute uncertainty in Beijing about potential future U.S. capability development leads to worst-case thinking about nuclear scenarios.

China and Russia team up against a common strategic foe. Shared concerns about strategic stability drive Russia and China to cooperate. Russia gets over its irritation about limited Chinese support during the war. The two countries coordinate to counter U.S. nuclear policies. They launch joint efforts to develop technologies to counter U.S. BMD. The strategic ties between the two countries grow. By the end of the decade, the two powers are much closer than they were in the immediate postwar period, but without wartime cooperation, are not as close as in Future 1. Cooperation between Beijing and Moscow in Future 3 is, however, deeper on nuclear and related technologies than in Future 2 because of concerns about strategic stability.

Divisions persist within NATO over postwar strategy. As in Future 1, NATO allies have a variety of views on the hardline approach toward Russia that the United States adopts after the war. However, in Future 3, these divisions persist throughout the decade. France and Germany, for example, point to Russia's weakness and question the need for a military buildup in Eastern Europe. Although these Western allies do not condone Russia's nuclear signaling, meddling in the politics of states along its periphery, or gray zone activities, they see U.S. policies as exacerbating these dynamics.

Allies can afford to spend more on defense in this future than in Futures 1 and 2 because their economies were not as deeply affected by the war. However, some allies have a less acute assessment of the threat Russia poses because of the state of its military at the end of the war. Therefore, those allies spend less on defense than they initially planned early in the war.

Russia-West economic decoupling gains steam in the postwar period. In this future, the West had not placed sanctions on China during the war, so the extent of global economic fragmentation is lower at the outset of the postwar decade than in Futures 1 and 2. As in all futures, the experience of unprecedented wartime sanctions on Russia convinces Beijing and Moscow that they need to continue to reduce their economic vulnerability. The nuclear arms race and political tensions accelerate Russia and China's efforts to reduce their dependence on the West.

Although the West lifted some sanctions during ceasefire negotiations, Russia is still much more economically isolated from the West than before the 2022 invasion. U.S.- and European-based companies and investors do not see Russia as an attractive partner because of continued Western sanctions, wartime nationalizations of Western-owned firms in Russia, and Russia's weak economy. The strategic-level U.S.-Russia tensions make the reimposition of sanctions appear likely, compounding private-sector reluctance to rebuild ties. Instead, firms see Russia's isolation as a feature of the postwar—not just wartime—setting.

The tensions with Moscow and Beijing accelerate the U.S. policy of derisking with such steps as export controls that have the effect of reducing economic ties with Russia and China over time.[20] However, the United States does not gain much support in Europe for reducing economic ties with China because, unlike in Future 1, Beijing did not undertake policies that deeply alienated U.S. European allies (e.g., supporting Russia militarily during the war). Over the decade after the war, the level of economic activity between rivals is higher than in Future 1, when all parties had the strongest wartime and postwar motivations to reduce reliance on one another, and lower than in Future 2. Ultimately, the effect is modest and far from total economic decoupling of the rival blocs.

---

[20] For a discussion of the Biden administration's de-risking strategy, see Agathe Demarais, "What Does 'De-Risking' Actually Mean?" *Foreign Policy*, August 23, 2023.

Future 4: Cold Peace

After the **more favorable war outcome**, the United States feels optimistic that Europe may become more stable. As part of the negotiations that ended the fighting, Russia and Ukraine have agreed to a robust ceasefire that appears durable. Hoping to build on this progress and stabilize the bilateral relationship, the United States adopts a **less hardline approach** toward Russia when the war is over (see Box 4.7). In the decade that follows, Europe settles into a cold peace, during which NATO-Russia and Russia-Ukraine tensions remain but the risk of conflict is lower than in any of the other futures (for a summary of these dynamics, see Box 4.8).

U.S. Motive: Stabilize Europe

Ukraine fared relatively well in the war, Russia has emerged significantly weaker in terms of its military power, and the Kremlin has signaled through its negotiating behavior that it has been somewhat chastened by the conflict. U.S. leaders take the view that the United States should give peace a chance and see whether the ceasefire can be a first step in a longer-term process of reestablishing stability in Europe.

This hopeful view does not mean that U.S. leaders expect to fundamentally transform the U.S.-Russia relationship or return to the status quo antebellum. Moscow's aggression and wartime atrocities have not been forgotten, and Moscow still has not taken responsibility for them. Still, the United States decides that its interests are not served by kicking Russia while it is down as it does in Future 3. As in the early Biden administration, the U.S. goal is "a stable, predictable relationship" with Russia. However, postwar bilateral relations are in a far worse state than they were in 2021.[21] Nonetheless, for Washington, reducing the risk of another war and creating the possibility of a return to more-normal bilateral relations are important strategic benefits, justifying the modest concessions required to achieve such relations.

---

[21] Joseph R. Biden, Jr., "Remarks by President Biden on Russia," White House, April 15, 2021.

BOX 4.7
Future 4: Postwar World and U.S. Strategy

World B: After the More Favorable War	Less Hardline Approach
War outcomes • The war ends soon • China does not provide Russia with lethal aid • The war ends in a robust ceasefire • Ukraine makes modest territorial gains **Strategic setting in the immediate aftermath of the war** • Russia is primarily security-motivated • Russia is severely weakened by the war and its defense industry is struggling • Russia-China relations are somewhat strained • Ukraine is focused on economic recovery • Ukraine's economy is significantly harmed by the war • NATO maintained unity on wartime policy toward Russia and Ukraine • U.S. shift to the Indo-Pacific region is not significantly limited by the war in Europe • The war does not have a major impact on U.S.-China tensions • Russia is much less economically integrated with the West	**Strategic stability** • Open to arms control negotiations • Restraint on nuclear weapons policy • Open to limits on U.S. BMD • Open to limits on intermediate-range ground-based missiles in Europe **Military presence in Europe** • Draw down forces • No additional forces to Eastern Europe • Open to talks on CFE-like limitations **Security relationship with Ukraine** • Provide assistance for a defensive posture and resiliency • Do not integrate Ukraine's military into NATO • Open to Ukraine's neutrality, no promotion of NATO membership **Policy toward other non-NATO former Soviet states** • No steps toward Georgia's NATO integration or membership • Reduce security cooperation with regional states • Limit efforts to undermine Russian influence **Economic relations with Russia** • Open to conditional sanctions relief

Key Postwar Dynamics

Ukraine adopts a porcupine strategy with U.S. support. Unlike in Future 2, the United States does not have to work as hard to convince Ukraine to adopt a porcupine strategy. Rather, such a strategy is consistent with Kyiv's desires

---

BOX 4.8
Key Dynamics in Future 4: Cold Peace

- Ukraine adopts a porcupine strategy with U.S. support.
- Ukraine respects the ceasefire.
- Allies support Ukraine's defense-oriented rearming.
- Ukraine chooses armed neutrality over integration with NATO.
- Allies' economic aid and support for EU integration help fuel Ukraine's economy.
- Moscow's obsession with Ukraine fades.
- Russia-Ukraine talks result in tangible, though limited, progress.
- There is a relatively stable new normal in other non-NATO former Soviet states.
- U.S.-Russia strategic-level tensions ease.
- Europe is stable, but the new dividing line between Russia and the West is here to stay.
- Russia seeks to consolidate control in occupied areas of Ukraine, not go on the offensive.
- Russia-China relations remain close.
- The global economy suffers minimal fragmentation.

---

to avoid another war and focus on economic development and recovery. The match between U.S. assistance and Kyiv's strategy makes Ukraine, by the end of the decade, a much harder—and thus less desirable—target for the Kremlin than in Future 2.

Ukraine respects the ceasefire. Ukraine stays the course on rebuilding and development even as continuing Russian occupation of swathes of its southeast create pressures within the country to continue the fight. The prospect of greater EU integration, facilitated by both the peace itself and Ukraine's reform drive, denies the hawks opportunities to build political support, and they largely remain marginal in Kyiv.

Allies support Ukraine's defense-oriented rearming. NATO allies provide the most substantial support to Ukraine to rearm in this future. Some NATO allies in Eastern Europe, especially Poland, oppose limits on the capabilities that the United States helps Ukraine develop. But these countries see little hope in lobbying for change given the consistency between Ukraine's own preferences and U.S. strategy. Although Poland and other countries also prefer a different strategy toward Russia, they are no less motivated to help Ukraine rearm and rebuild because of the tactical dispute with Washington. Kyiv's focus on recovery and democracy makes Paris and Berlin more supportive of Ukraine than in Futures 1 and 2.

Ukraine chooses armed neutrality over integration with NATO. Several trends push the ever-present specter of Ukraine's NATO membership into the background. Kyiv itself embraced neutrality to get the deal that ended the war. The United States is not pushing Ukraine's NATO membership. And armed neutrality is working out well for the Ukrainians: Despite nonaligned status, Ukraine receives ample support from NATO allies for its defense-oriented strategy. With Russia less inclined to attack in this future, the benefits of this new status are seen to outweigh the loss of the prospect for membership, particularly because the path to joining had never been clear.

Allies' economic aid and support for EU integration help fuel Ukraine's economy. As in Future 3, the European economy's relatively better state after the shorter war leaves the EU with the resources to support a Ukraine that is strengthening its democratic institutions. As in Future 3, EU membership for Ukraine is still elusive, but deeper integration proves transformative. Refugees and investors return as a result.

Russia's obsession with Ukraine fades. In this future, Russia's objectives in Ukraine are to prevent security threats emanating from Kyiv and maintain control over the territory that it occupied at the end of the war. Because Russia's goal of Ukrainian nonalignment was achieved during the armistice talks and reinforced by Ukraine's postwar policies, Moscow no longer feels compelled to completely control decisionmaking in Kyiv, and the Russian military's inability to secure further territory underscores the tremendous cost of pursuing that goal. As it becomes clear that NATO is not pushing to integrate Ukraine and the United States limits the types of capabilities provided to Kyiv, Russia's concerns diminish further. The Kremlin still harbors dreams of bringing Ukraine to heel, but these dreams do not drive policy. Instead, Russia focuses on the basics of rebuilding its force after the losses in the war and the revelation of so many weaknesses. This rearming does not focus solely on a future war with Ukraine but rather on improving Russian capabilities against a variety of threats. Moreover, without either a domestic

Ukrainian drive for a near-term resumption of hostilities or acute fears of NATO enlargement, Russia demobilizes some of its forces and devotes fewer resources to defense than in the other scenarios.

Russia-Ukraine talks result in tangible, though limited, progress. The two countries engage in a political dialogue established during the cease-fire talks, but there is little progress on a comprehensive settlement. The mutual hostility from the war remains, as do the sides' irreconcilable territorial claims. Russia and Ukraine instead focus on narrower issues, much as they did during the war itself when discrete deals were reached on grain exports and prisoner exchanges. In the postwar context, discussions lead to agreements on such issues as freedom of movement (a limited easing of state border restrictions, plus some humanitarian access across the LoC) and a gradual partial resumption of trade.

There is a relatively stable new normal in other non-NATO former Soviet states. U.S. restraint on Russia's periphery gives a weakened and security-minded Kremlin less incentive to lash out at its other neighbors. An uneasy new normal sets in that sees the continuing gradual waning of Russian influence everywhere except Belarus. Moscow tries to arrest this slide but has few tools to do so, given its weakened clout after the war.

U.S.-Russia strategic-level tensions ease. In the years that follow the war, there is a mutual ratcheting down of threat perceptions after the terms of the armistice stick and interactions, such as the U.S.-Russia strategic stability dialogue, resume.

Russia's return to implementation of the NST at the end of the war facilitates arms control negotiations. A successor treaty is eventually signed and enters into force; in parallel, NATO-Russia talks produce new, politically binding conventional and theater-strike restraint measures for Europe. The United States announces a more restrained plan for future BMD interceptor deployments and commits not to exceed it. Although Russia feels vulnerable in its conventional weakness, U.S willingness to engage in nuclear and conventional arms control stabilizes the bilateral strategic dynamic, leading to a relatively restrained Russian posture. Russia is not increasing its numbers of tactical nuclear weapons, nor is it expanding the geography of its deployments because conflict with NATO seems less likely in this future. U.S. restraint on the strategic side has minimized the incentives for a Russian buildup in terms of warheads or delivery systems—or for saber-rattling.

Europe is stable, but the new dividing line between Russia and the West is here to stay. Rather than the unilateral drawdown of forces in Future 2, in this future, Washington is, together with its NATO allies, able to reach a deal with Moscow on conventional forces in Europe. This agreement prevents a military buildup on either side of the NATO-Russia border, limiting the forces that can be deployed within a specified area. These limits affect those capabilities that could be used to enable surprise attack.[22] The agreement also restores confidence- and security-building measures (CSBMs), including mutual inspections, that had essentially ceased even before the war. Despite the drawdown, U.S. security engagement in Europe is still significant.

NATO allies were spooked by Russia's aggression during the war and remain willing to spend more for their own defense than before the war, and they have more resources to do so than in Futures 1 and 2 because their economies were not as affected by the shorter war. Still, the less acute threat perceptions in the postwar period mean that allies do not spend as much as they projected during the war itself.

Divisions on postwar policy among allies do exist as they do in Future 2, but all are committed to collective defense. In this future, there is more unity in the alliance because even the hardliners see the Russia threat as less acute than it was in wartime. That said, the war has permanently hardened attitudes toward Russia across the continent. Moscow will remain excluded from the major organizations determining the future of European security—NATO and the EU.

Russia seeks to consolidate control in occupied areas of Ukraine, not go on the offensive. Without the imperialist motive and with the situation in Ukraine more or less stable, Russia does not invest as much in forces for another offensive. Rather, it focuses on holding the territory that it already controls.

Russia-China relations remain close. Although Russia is somewhat irritated with China for having limited its wartime support, Moscow still benefits from close relations with its neighbor. Unprecedented Western

---

[22] For examples of such capabilities, see Samuel Charap, Alice Lynch, John J. Drennan, Dara Massicot, and Giacomo Persi Paoli, *A New Approach to Conventional Arms Control in Europe: Addressing the Security Challenges of the 21st Century*, RAND Corporation, RR-4346, 2020.

wartime sanctions reinforced Russia's desire to build alternative financial and trading arrangements and limit its exposure to Western markets. These incentives remain even as some sanctions ease in the postwar period. As when the United States had adopted a less hardline approach and tensions had eased somewhat in the past, Moscow still sees the United States as the most significant threat to its security.[23]

Never knowing when the West might try to use economic tools coercively again, Russia continues to hedge against a future conflict by taking such steps as investing in infrastructure for gas exports to China. Russia sustains security ties with China, and the countries remain far more closely linked militarily than prior to 2022. But because threats from the West have moderated, this future creates fewer incentives than in the others for Moscow to double down on those ties. Ultimately, Russia-China relations plateau.

The global economy suffers minimal fragmentation. Russia is certainly more economically isolated from Europe than before the war. But given the lifting of some sanctions and as it becomes clear that the situation in Ukraine is stabilizing, Europe-Russia trade resumes to some degree. Because Beijing did not support Moscow during the conflict, the United States and its allies did not sanction China. Russia and China, as noted previously, continue their steps to reduce their reliance on the West and vulnerability to future sanctions, but do so more slowly than in other futures in which their threat perceptions were more acute. Similarly, compared with Futures 1 and 2—which feature elevated U.S.-China nuclear tensions—the United States has fewer motivations to bear the costs of policies aimed at reducing economic integration with China. Overall, therefore, economic relations among rivals are more integrated than in the other futures.

---

[23] For detailed discussions of these historical episodes, see Priebe, Frederick, Evans, et al., 2023.

CHAPTER 5

Implications for U.S. Interests

In this chapter, we compare the implications of these four alternative futures for U.S. interests. While U.S. policymakers cannot select a preferred future, their wartime decisions can have *some* impact on the outcome of the war, and policymakers do have full control over the choice of postwar strategy. In other words, U.S. policy can help enable the future that best serves U.S. interests.

We begin by outlining a methodology for assessing the implications of the four futures for U.S. interests. We then consider how the dynamics in each future affect these interests.

U.S. Interests

There is no consensus on U.S. interests in either academic political science or the policy debate. Therefore, we begin by explaining our choice of U.S. interests for our assessment; specifically, the U.S. position in the global distribution of power, avoiding a major power conflict, the strength of the U.S. economy, Ukraine's security and prosperity, and minimizing conflict risk in other non-NATO former Soviet states.

U.S. position in the global distribution of power. Strategists debate how globally and regionally dominant the United States needs to be to defend its interests. But existing U.S. grand strategy sees defending allies and partners in Europe and Asia as a key U.S. interest. Therefore, we consider the conventional military power that the United States can bring to bear to deter aggression and, if necessary, wage war to defend friendly states in these regions.[1] We also compare U.S. nuclear weapon capability with Russia's and China's.

Avoiding a major power conflict. U.S. policymakers and outside strategists generally agree that the most vital U.S. interest is the security of the homeland.[2] In both postwar worlds, the United States will still be the most militarily powerful state in the international system and, because of its capabilities and geography, incredibly secure. Still, in the event of a major power conflict, Russia and China both have capabilities to strike the U.S. homeland (e.g., cyber, nuclear). Therefore, such a war would be a threat to the most vital U.S. interest. Moreover, great power war could lead to major loss of life and military capabilities, as well as economic damage.

Strength of the U.S. economy. We consider how dynamics in our futures affect U.S. economic growth because the health of the U.S. economy is the long-term basis of U.S. power and affects the quality of all Americans' lives.

Ukraine's security and prosperity. We also consider those U.S. regional interests that are most likely to be affected by postwar dynamics. In particular, ensuring Ukraine's security and prosperity is a key consideration for the United States. To assess this interest, we consider the possibility of another Russia-Ukraine war, Ukraine's ability to defend itself, the strength of the country's economy, and the health of its democracy.

Minimizing conflict risk in other non-NATO former Soviet states. We also consider how postwar dynamics affect the risk of conflict in other former Soviet, non-NATO countries in Eastern Europe and the South Caucasus: Armenia, Azerbaijan, Belarus, Georgia, and Moldova. We do so because these states are the most likely loci of potential future Russian interventions in light of its past behavior, most vividly demonstrated in its invasion of Ukraine. We do not consider effects in post-Soviet Central Asia, which would, to a greater degree, require assumptions about China's activities in the region that are outside the scope of this report. Avoiding another destabilizing war will be important for the United States after this one ends.

---

[1] Joseph R. Biden, Jr., *National Security Strategy*, White House, October 2022.

[2] See, for example, Biden, 2022, p. 7; Daryl Press, *Calculating Credibility: How Leaders Assess Military Threats*, Cornell University Press, 2005, pp. 25–28; and Posen, 2014.

U.S. Position in the Global Distribution of Power

The United States would remain the most conventionally capable global military power in all four futures. However, some of the dynamics in the futures could affect U.S. nuclear capabilities relative to those of its primary adversaries, Russia and China, as well as the conventional military balance in Europe and Asia, the two regions where those adversaries' military forces are concentrated and where competition is most intense. Figure 5.1 summarizes the differences across futures that we detail in the following sections.

Nuclear Capabilities

There is no consensus in the literature on how to assess the nuclear balance or even on the utility of doing so. Policymakers and analysts have measured the nuclear balance in many ways, including by making simple quantitative comparisons of warheads and delivery systems and developing more-complex models of each state's ability to destroy specific targets. Beyond questions about how to measure the nuclear balance, there is significant debate about whether the balance matters when it comes to the top nuclear powers. Analysts disagree about whether, after having achieved an assured retaliation capability, a state's ability to deter and coerce others increases with greater numbers of weapons.[3] Policy discussions often emphasize the value of a larger nuclear force to U.S. security.[4] However, there is no schol-

---

[3] For a recent summary of these debates, see David C. Logan, "The Nuclear Balance Is What States Make of It," *International Security*, Vol. 46, No. 4, Spring 2022. For more detailed discussions, see Matthew Kroenig, "Nuclear Superiority and the Balance of Resolve: Explaining Nuclear Crisis Outcomes," *International Organization*, Vol. 67, No. 1, Winter 2013; Mark S. Bell and Julia Macdonald, "How to Think About Nuclear Crises (February 2019)," *Texas National Security Review*, Vol. 2, No. 2, February 2019; Keir A. Lieber and Daryl G. Press, "The Rise of U.S. Nuclear Primacy," *Foreign Affairs*, Vol. 85, No. 2, March–April 2006; and Todd S. Sechser and Matthew Fuhrmann, "Crisis Bargaining and Nuclear Blackmail," *International Organization*, Vol. 67, No. 1, Winter 2013.

[4] See, for example, Madelyn R. Creedon, Jon L. Kyl, Marshall S. Billingslea, Gloria C. Duffy, Rose E. Gottemoeller, Lisa E. Gordon-Hagerty, Rebeccah L. Heinrichs, John E. Hyten, Robert M. Scher, Matthew H. Kroenig, Franklin C. Miller, and Leonor A. Tomero, *America's Strategic Posture: The Final Report of the Congressional Commission*

FIGURE 5.1

Key Measures of U.S. Power Relative to Pre-War Trends

	Future 1: Pervasive Instability	Future 2: Localized Instability	Future 3: Cold War 2.0	Future 4: Cold Peace
U.S. assured retaliation capability				
Distribution of power in Europe	✓	✓✓	✓✓✓	✓✓✓✓
Distribution of power in Asia	✗✗✗	✗✗	✗✗✗	✗

NOTE: Blank gray cells indicate no effect. Green cells and checkmarks indicate that there are benefits for U.S. interests relative to pre-war trends. Red cells and crosses indicate worse outcomes. Darker shades and more checks or crosses represent larger differences. See the text for assumptions and uncertainties associated with these rough assessments.

arly agreement on whether China and Russia building more weapons or having a more modernized force would reduce U.S. security as long as the United States retains an assured retaliation capability.

There are also analytical challenges to assessing the nuclear balance in our futures. To do so, we would need to make detailed projections about how each country carries out its modernization program and how various qualitative improvements and quantitative increases net out over a decade. The events described in our futures would not be the main driver of these dynamics and thus offer no clear guide to making such projections. Therefore, we focus on the narrow but core issue of the effect of the dynamics in each future on the key powers' assured retaliation capabilities, which analysts agree is the foundation of nuclear deterrence.

Before the war, China had already initiated a major nuclear buildup and modernization program.[5] The United States and Russia were modernizing

---

on the Strategic Posture of the United States, Institute for Defense Analyses, October 2023.

[5] The U.S. Department of Defense believes China's nuclear buildup began in 2021 (U.S. Department of Defense, *Military and Security Developments Involving the People's Republic of China, Annual Report to Congress,* November 29, 2022d).

but not significantly expanding their nuclear forces.[6] In Futures 1 and 3, the end of U.S.-Russia arms control and other dynamics accelerate the U.S. qualitative and quantitative arms race with Russia and China. In Futures 2 and 4, there is far less arms-racing pressure, although a return to the pre-war prospects of more ambitious arms control and even reductions is off the table due to the demise of the NST and the downturn in relations.

Effects on U.S. assured retaliation capability. The dynamics in Futures 1 and 3 are unlikely to undermine the U.S. assured retaliation capability. Eliminating or even weakening the U.S. second strike capability would take more than numbers: It would require a technological breakthrough by Russia or China. For example, to threaten the survivability of U.S. SSBNs, China and Russia would need to develop the ability to detect, track, and destroy these submarines. The challenges of doing so remain formidable.[7] The United States also uses tactics, technology, and quantity to make the other two legs of the nuclear triad—bombers and ICBMs— survivable. Therefore, to undermine the security of the U.S. second strike capability, China and Russia would need to have forces capable of threatening all three legs of the U.S. nuclear triad. Russia and China were presumably already working on such capabilities prior to the war.[8] The increased investment in and Russia-China cooperation on such efforts resulting from the dynamics in Futures 1 and 3 could lead to more technological progress

---

[6] Hans M. Kristensen, Matt Korda, and Eliana Johns, "Nuclear Notebook: Russian Nuclear Weapons, 2023," *Bulletin of the Atomic Scientists*, Vol. 79, No. 3, 2023; Hans M. Kristensen, Matt Korda, Eliana Johns, and Kate Kohn, "Status of World Nuclear Forces," Federation of American Scientists, March 31, 2023.

[7] Ryan Snyder, Benoît Pelopidas, Keir A. Lieber, and Daryl G. Press, "Correspondence: New Era or New Error? Technology and the Future of Deterrence," *International Security*, Vol. 43, No. 3, Winter 2018–2019; Sarah Kirchberger, "Obstacles and Breakthroughs in China's Defense Technological Development: China's Undersea Warfare," testimony before the U.S.-China Economic and Security Review Commission, April 13, 2023; Rory Medcalf, Katherine Mansted, Stephan Frühling, and James Goldrick, eds., *The Future of the Undersea Deterrent: A Global Survey*, Australian National University, National Security College, Indo-Pacific Strategy Series, February 2020.

[8] For a discussion of how technological developments already underway are affecting the survivability of nuclear forces, see Keir A. Lieber and Daryl G. Press, "The New Era of Counterforce: Technological Change and the Future of Nuclear Deterrence," *International Security*, Vol. 41, No. 4, Spring 2017.

and increase the likelihood of a breakthrough. But it is ultimately unlikely that they can deploy capabilities that overcome U.S. countermeasures on all three legs of the nuclear triad within a decade.

Effects on Russia and China's assured retaliation capabilities. In Futures 1 and 3, the United States spends more both to increase the quantity of deployed nuclear warheads and on innovations to detect, track, and destroy its rivals' warheads and delivery systems. This could increase the likelihood of a U.S. breakthrough that could undermine China or Russia's assured retaliation capability (and that may not have occurred absent the dynamics in Futures 1 and 3). However, such an outcome is unlikely since the United States would be up against multiple challenges. Both countries already have sophisticated programs to secure their second strike capabilities (e.g., road-mobile missiles, SSBNs) and would make determined efforts to sustain their second strike capabilities during an arms race. Moreover, U.S. strategy is oriented around the nuclear programs of both rivals, so the United States cannot focus all its resources on one adversary. Finally, in these futures, there are increasing incentives for Russia and China to cooperate on technology to prevent U.S. nuclear primacy. The dynamics in these futures are therefore unlikely to result in the United States having the ability to threaten the assured retaliation capabilities of either or both countries.

Although we are skeptical that the United States could *actually* fully undermine these countries' assured retaliation capabilities, in the following sections, we discuss how the dynamics in these futures could affect Russia and China's *perceptions* of the risk that the United States achieves nuclear primacy.

Distribution of Power in Europe

U.S. military power relative to Russia's is a function of both sides' military capabilities and the capabilities that each side's allies and partners would bring to bear in the event of conflict. In all four futures, the United States and its NATO allies taken together are unquestionably conventionally stronger relative to Russia at the end of the war and throughout the postwar decade. Yet differences in war outcomes and postwar dynamics mean that that the extent of U.S. advantages varies across the futures.

For each future, we describe the multiple dynamics that affect the distribution of power. Net assessment of these sometimes countervailing trends is challenging. Dynamics in the futures cannot always easily be weighed on the same scale (e.g., combat losses versus economic effects that could affect defense spending). We have greater confidence about the direction of effects than their magnitude, complicating attempts to compare countervailing dynamics. For example, reductions in economic growth should limit Russia's ability to spend on defense, but we do not have a strong basis for predicting how much this would be offset by increases in lethal aid from China. We attempt to make a rough net assessment of these effects in each future, but given the challenges, we note significant uncertainty about our judgments.

Future 1

Prior to the Russia-Ukraine war, NATO was conventionally more capable than Russia. In Future 1, several dynamics further favor the United States and its allies. Most importantly, Russia's military power erodes over the course of the war. And its economy—the long-term basis of its power—suffers from sanctions. Moreover, growing global economic fragmentation hurts Russia's economy more than those of the United States and its allies.[9] In addition to the factors dragging on Russia, the United States sustains its wartime force levels in Europe and continues investing in capabilities for a possible war in in the region. NATO allies, especially in Eastern Europe, also spend more on defense than expected before the war (Table 5.1).

Other dynamics in Future 1 favor Russia: Its reinvigorated defense industry and support from China during and after the war help it recover. The de facto alliance with China also means that in the event of a NATO-Russia conflict, Beijing is more likely to, at a minimum, provide Moscow with

---

[9] For research that finds the Russian economy would suffer more from decoupling than those of the United States and its allies, see Gabriel Felbermayr, Hendrik Mahlkow, and Alexander Sandkamp, "Cutting Through the Value Chain: The Long-Run Effects of Decoupling the East from the West," *Empirica: Journal of European Economics*, Vol. 50, No. 1, February 2023. For related findings for fragmentation in commodity markets, see International Monetary Fund, 2023.

lethal aid.[10] Given increasing tensions with the United States, Russia also shifts resources toward capabilities for a high-end fight with NATO—e.g., anti-satellite weapons, cruise missiles—and the nuclear arms race.

One remaining dynamic is likely to favor Russia, but the size of this effect is particularly unclear. Early in the postwar period, there are deep disagreements within NATO about postwar strategy: Some allies see the hardline U.S. strategy as excessively provocative toward Russia. As a result, some allies are less committed to NATO as an institution and to foster-ing close ties with the United States generally. It is difficult to know how such peacetime dynamics would translate to behavior if NATO allies were directly involved in a war.[11] There has never been a NATO-Russia war, so we do not have a historical basis for predicting whether allies would come to one another's defense if they believed an ally's policy was a significant cause

TABLE 5.1

How Future 1 Dynamics Affect the European Distribution of Power Relative to Pre-War Trends

Favors the United States	Favors Russia
• Russia's wartime military losses • Larger U.S. presence in Europe • Increased defense spending by NATO member-states • Russia suffers more economically from sanctions and increasing economic fragmentation than NATO countries do	• Rejuvenated Russian defense industry • Increased Russian investment in high-end capabilities for a war with NATO • China's wartime support to Russia's military • Higher likelihood that China would provide lethal aid in the event of a future NATO-Russia war • Temporary reduction in some NATO allies' commitments to collective defense in the postwar period

---

[10] For the factors that China might consider when deciding how much to support Russia, see Liana Fix and Michael Kimmage, "How China Could Save Putin's War in Ukraine: The Logic—and Consequences—of Chinese Military Support for Russia," *Foreign Affairs*, April 26, 2023.

[11] For a more detailed discussion of such dynamics, see Anika Binnendijk and Miranda Priebe, *An Attack Against Them All? Drivers of Decisions to Contribute to NATO Collective Defense*, RAND Corporation, RR-2964-OSD, 2019.

of the war. In the extreme, some allies could choose not to fight and refuse to provide U.S. and other allied forces access to its territory. Depending on the ally, loss of access could significantly affect allied power projection. For example, if Germany did not allow U.S. forces to operate from its soil, the defense of Eastern European allies would be much more difficult. In a less extreme outcome, some key allies might allow access, but choose to not contribute forces, resulting in a more modest reduction in the capabilities that NATO could bring to bear in wartime. However, given NATO's overwhelming advantages and the fact that the U.S. military remains the backbone of the alliance's power, a few allies' decisions not to contribute would not dramatically change the military balance. In short, peacetime divisions early in the postwar period could raise questions about commitment to collective defense but would significantly alter the distribution of power in Europe only if key allies refused access to U.S. and other allies' forces. Over the course of the postwar decade, however, Russia's provocative actions cause allies to come to a shared view of the threat that it poses. Therefore, these concerns about commitment to collective defense diminish by the end of the decade.

On net, these countervailing dynamics are unlikely to be significant enough to overcome NATO's material advantages relative to Russia in Europe, especially given NATO's pre-war advantages and Russia's wartime losses.

Future 2

As in Future 1, Russia's military is bolstered by a rejuvenated domestic defense industry, wartime support from China and, with closer ties, a greater likelihood that China would provide significant support in the event of a NATO-Russia war (see Table 5.2).

In Future 2, the United States reduces deployments in Europe back to pre-war levels. However, this policy choice would not necessarily directly translate into lower U.S. relative power in Europe compared with Future 1. There are fewer political tensions in Europe in this future, and the U.S. posture is less threatening to Russia (e.g., no intermediate-range missiles deployed, fewer forces in Eastern Europe). So Russia would be less motivated to invest in high-end capabilities for a conflict with NATO and militarize the NATO-Russia border. Instead, facing a diminished threat from NATO, we expect that Moscow would focus on rebuilding its military to support

TABLE 5.2

How Future 2 Dynamics Affect the European Distribution of Power Relative to Pre-War Trends

Favors NATO	Favors Russia
• Russia's wartime losses • Increased defense spending by NATO member-states • Russia suffers more economically from sanctions and increasing economic fragmentation than NATO countries do	• Rejuvenated Russian defense industry • China's wartime support to Russia's military • Higher likelihood that China provides lethal aid in the event of a future NATO-Russia war

a future ground campaign in Ukraine to satisfy its imperialist ambitions. Therefore, the U.S. drawdown does not have a significant negative effect on the distribution of power relevant to a high-end NATO-Russia war.

Several dynamics favor the United States and NATO as in Future 1: Russia is weakened by combat losses and can spend modestly less on defense because of the effects of growing global economic fragmentation. Moreover, allies spend more on defense than expected before the war.

In addition to a strong material position in Future 2, NATO allies remain committed to collective defense in the postwar period. This could mean that, throughout the decade after the war, allies would be confident in bringing more of the alliance's power to bear in the event of a NATO-Russia conflict (compared with Future 1, in which there are questions about key allies' commitment early in the postwar period).

Future 3

As in Future 1, the United States sustains a larger military presence in Europe after the war. Moreover, Russia is even weaker at the end of the war than in Futures 1 and 2 because it did not receive lethal aid from China and its defense industry was not rejuvenated (see Table 5.3).

Cutting in the other direction, the intense competition with the United States leads Russia to spend more on preparations for a high-end fight, although it has fewer resources to do so than in Future 1. Still, China appears just as likely to support Russia in the event of a war with NATO. Some allies in Western Europe have less acute threat perceptions, given Russia's weakness, so spend less than in Futures 1 and 2. Questions about collective defense emerge, as in Future 1, since some allies see U.S. policies as need-

TABLE 5.3

How Future 3 Dynamics Affect the European Distribution of Power Relative to Pre-War Trends

Favors NATO	Favors Russia
• Russia's wartime losses • Larger U.S. presence in Europe • NATO allies spend somewhat more on defense • Russia suffers more economically from sanctions and increasing economic fragmentation than NATO countries do	• Russia rebuilds capabilities for a high-end fight but with a weaker defense industry • High likelihood that China provides lethal aid in the event of a future NATO-Russia war • Some NATO allies' commitment to collective defense weakens

lessly provocative. Unlike in Future 1, these questions persist throughout the decade, creating the possibility that some allies may not provide access to U.S. forces during a NATO-Russia war or fight in such a war themselves.

It is difficult to compare these outcomes with those in Futures 1 and 2. But Russia's greater weakness at the end of the war would likely outweigh allies' somewhat lower defense spending and questions surrounding collective defense. Therefore the regional power balance could be somewhat more favorable for the United States in Future 3 than in Futures 1 and 2, although we have low confidence in this assessment.

Future 4

As in Future 2, the United States reduces its forces in Europe, but this does not significantly affect the regional distribution of power because Russia does not invest as much in high-end capabilities for a NATO-Russia war because political and military tensions are lower. As in Future 3, some Western NATO allies spend less on defense than they committed to do during the war, since they assess that Russia poses less of a threat given its weakness (see Table 5.4).

As in Future 3, Russia came out of the shorter war even weaker than NATO. But, in this future, Russia rebuilds its military at a slower pace because its security concerns are less acute and it does not have the strong imperialist drive. Although some Eastern European allies disagree with the less hardline U.S. approach, they remain deeply committed to NATO, and commitment to collective defense remains high. Russia and China are closer than they were before the war, but ten years out, the Russia-China axis is less

TABLE 5.4

How Future 4 Dynamics Affect the European Distribution of Power Relative to Pre-War Trends

Favors NATO	Favors Russia
• Russia's wartime losses • NATO allies spend somewhat more on defense than before the war • Russia suffers more economically from sanctions and increasing economic fragmentation than NATO countries do	• High likelihood that China provides lethal aid in the event of a future NATO-Russia war

close than in any of the other futures. On net, therefore, this future could yield the most favorable power balance in Europe for the United States.

Distribution of Power in Asia

The U.S.-China distribution of power in the decade after the war will largely be a function of factors beyond those discussed in the futures. But some dynamics we describe could have an impact. To assess the effect of the war on U.S. relative power in the Indo-Pacific, we make a few assumptions. First, we assume that but for the Russia-Ukraine war, the United States would have continued its policy of gradually shifting resources to the Indo-Pacific region. Second, we assume that in all futures, the U.S. defense budget will at most gradually increase, not dramatically expand.[12] Finally, given the stated U.S. prioritization of the Indo-Pacific region in its latest national security strategy, we assume that any resources that the United States moves away from Europe would shift to the Indo-Pacific region rather than another theater or domestic priorities.[13] To the extent that the U.S. defense budget is constrained, more resources devoted to Europe means fewer resources available in the Indo-Pacific region.

In all futures, the United States diverts funds to Europe to support Ukraine, U.S. allies, and a larger U.S. presence in the region. Therefore, the

---

[12] This assumption is consistent with projections from the Congressional Budget Office based on current DoD plans (David Arthur and F. Matthew Woodward, *Long-Term Implications of the 2023 Future Years Defense Program*, Congressional Budget Office, January 2023, p. 2).

[13] Biden, 2022.

resources the United States could have otherwise put toward the Indo-Pacific region are somewhat diminished. The magnitude of this trade-off requires comparing resources devoted to Europe with pre-war trends, which we are unable to assess. Still, we can point to reasons why the effect on U.S. power in the Indo-Pacific region would vary across the futures.

In Futures 1 and 3, the United States adopts a hardline strategy that requires more U.S. resources in Europe for a larger military presence than before the war. These futures also see more-intense NATO-Russia competition, which means the United States would likely also expend resources to prepare for the higher likelihood of major power war in the region. Therefore, the hardline strategy leaves fewer resources for the Indo-Pacific.

In addition to limiting U.S. resource shifts to the Indo-Pacific, dynamics in these futures could also contribute to China's military power. Heightened Russia-China security cooperation in Futures 1 and 3, including joint military development and technology transfers, would likely modestly help Beijing continue its buildup, especially in such key areas as evading U.S. BMD, nuclear modernization, and submarine technology. Russia and China's deepening ties make it more likely that Moscow would provide support in any future U.S.-China war than it might have considered before the 2022 invasion. As a result, U.S. power declines relative to China's in Futures 1 and 3, though the size of this effect, as noted previously, would depend on how many resources the United States diverted to Europe.

In Future 2, the United States reduces the number of forces deployed in Europe as part of the less hardline strategy. Moreover, the risk of a NATO-Russia war in Europe is lower in Future 2 than in Future 1, so the United States does not need to spend as much on preparations for a conflict in Europe. Therefore, the United States can shift more resources to the Indo-Pacific than in Future 1. Still, another war in Ukraine remains plausible in Future 2, even though there are fewer pathways to that outcome. A war like the current one would carry an elevated risk of NATO-Russia conflict. Therefore, the United States may hesitate to fully pivot away from Europe by, for example, optimizing force structure for air and naval conflict in the Indo-Pacific region. Instead, the United States may hedge, keeping resources available to respond to contingencies in Europe and to deter Russian attacks on NATO member-states. The high risk of another conflict in Ukraine could thus have some consequences for generating military power in the Indo-Pacific. But there is a lower risk of a NATO-Russia war than in Futures 1 and 3 and, as a result, less of a negative effect on the military balance in Asia.

In Future 4, the United States draws down its forces in Europe as it does in Future 2. However, greater European stability in Future 4 allows the United States to commit to a deeper shift toward the Indo-Pacific, through such changes as optimizing force structure for that theater. The power balance vis-à-vis China is thus more favorable to the United States in this future than in the others.

Avoiding a Major Power Conflict

In this section, we consider the risk of U.S. involvement in a conflict with Russia or China. In addition to the possibility of conventional conflict, we examine the risk of nuclear war. Major power wars are rare, and nuclear use has not occurred since the end of World War II.[14] Still, such events would be highly consequential for the United States. Therefore, we discuss how the risks of such outcomes varies across futures, even as the absolute likelihood of these events would likely still be small (Figure 5.2).

Risk of Conventional Conflict with Russia

In assessing the risk of a conventional U.S.-Russia war, we assume that the United States would fight to defend any NATO member-state attacked by Moscow. There are several possible pathways to a NATO-Russia war:

- Russia launching an opportunistic war against a NATO member-state
- a U.S. attack on Russia aimed at regime change or disarming the country

---

[14] The number of interstate wars declined in recent decades, though there has been a significant uptick in the number of fatalities caused by interstate wars, such as the ongoing Russia-Ukraine war (Aaron Clauset, "Trends and Fluctuations in the Severity of Interstate Wars," *Science Advances*, Vol. 4, No. 2, February 2018; Shawn Davies, Thérése Pettersson, and Magnus Öberg, "Organized Violence 1989–2022, and the Return of Conflict Between States," *Journal of Peace Research*, Vol. 60, No. 4, July 2023).

- conflict that begins by misperception by either side
- escalation of another Russia-Ukraine war.

The first pathway to war is equally improbable across the four futures because NATO's deterrent has proven to be strong. Russia has not used force against a NATO country, even during the ongoing war when member-states have been providing significant support to Ukraine. Russia's relative weakness compared with the status quo ante bellum makes it even less likely that it would start an opportunistic war with NATO.

We also assess that the chance of the second pathway to conflict—an intentional U.S. attack on Russia aimed at regime change or disarming the country—would be equally low across the four futures. (That said, expansive U.S. goals could emerge in a conflict that begins for one of the other reasons we consider here.) Attacking the Russian homeland would create the near certainty of major power war, including a high risk of a strategic exchange. As we have seen since 2022, the Biden administration has even deemed fighting Russia in Ukraine to be too risky. Despite Russia's conventional weakness in certain futures, it would remain a nuclear weapons state with an assured retaliation capability. Even a much more hawkish U.S. administration is highly unlikely to court such a high risk of a nuclear war in any plausible future scenario. Therefore, we focus on assessing the remaining two pathways to a U.S.-Russia war.

Future 1. Political tensions remain high after the war as an imperialist Russia appears committed to future aggression, the United States supports Ukraine's integration with NATO and turns a blind eye to Kyiv's ceasefire violations, and bilateral arms control collapses.

In this context, military moves by either side could increase concerns about the other's intentions. The U.S. deployment of intermediate-range missiles to Europe exacerbates Russia's concerns about the United States targeting Russia's nuclear forces.[15] The movement of more U.S. forces east would likely also heighten Moscow's threat perceptions. With more forces operating in close proximity, the risk of military accidents increases too,

---

[15] Charap et al., 2020, pp. 30–33.

FIGURE 5.2

Risk of U.S. Involvement in a Major Power Conflict Relative to Pre-War Trends

	Future 1: Pervasive Instability	Future 2: Localized Instability	Future 3: Cold War 2.0	Future 4: Cold Peace
Risk of U.S.-Russia conventional conflict	✕✕✕✕	✕✕	✕✕✕	✕
Risk of U.S.-Russia nuclear conflict	✕✕✕	✕✕	✕✕✕✕	✕
Risk of U.S.-China nuclear conflict	✕✕✕	✕✕	✕✕✕	✕

NOTE: Darker red and more crosses represent worse outcomes compared with pre-war trends. See the text for assumptions and uncertainties associated with these rough assessments.

which could further increase tensions.[16] Although we assess that Russia is unlikely to pursue an opportunistic war against a NATO member-state, many allies already appear to fear such an attack.[17] Russia's militarization of its border with NATO and increased preparations for a high-end fight would likely exacerbate these concerns.

Great power war is costly and dangerous, so decisionmakers on both sides have incentives to prevent such dynamics from escalating. Conditions in Future 1, however, make managing tensions difficult. Communications between the United States and Russia are sparse as political tensions prevent the resumption of bilateral diplomatic dialogues that were shut down during the war. With threat perceptions heightened on both sides, each is

---

[16] Accidents are more likely to exacerbate tensions rather than act as an independent cause of war (Stephen L. Quackenbush, "The Problem with Accidental War," *Conflict Management and Peace Science*, Vol. 40, No. 6, November 2023; Marc Trachtenberg, "The 'Accidental War' Question," February 14, 2000). For a thorough review of the historiography of the Spanish-American War and why the argument that the sinking of the USS *Maine* caused an accidental war does not hold up to rigorous scrutiny, see Louis A. Pérez, "The Meaning of the Maine: Causation and the Historiography of the Spanish-American War," *Pacific Historical Review*, Vol. 58, No. 3, August 1989.

[17] Sinéad Baker and Jake Epstein, "Front-Line NATO Allies Worry They Could Be Next After Russia's Invasion of Ukraine and Are Getting Ready for a Fight," *Business Insider*, April 23, 2023.

more likely to assume the worst about the other's intent, making it harder for decisionmakers to use diplomacy to avert conflict.[18]

Still, for a war to begin, one side must decide to attack first. Because opportunistic aggression between nuclear powers is highly unlikely, we focus instead on the risk of an *anticipatory attack,* one initiated for defensive reasons in the belief that war is either likely imminent or likely to occur eventually. Such attacks can come in two forms: preventive or preemptive.[19] A *preemptive war* occurs when one side attacks to gain first mover advantages in the belief that war is imminent. A *preventive war* occurs when one side initiates conflict in response to a less imminent threat of conflict in the belief that fighting in the present moment is better than later. This occurs when a state faces an adverse shift in the distribution of power as a result of, for example, an adversary building up its military capabilities more quickly or an anticipated change in international alignment (e.g., alliance formation by the other side, potential loss of a state's own allies' support with time). When a state facing such an adverse shift believes that conflict (or another severe outcome, such as domination by another state) is likely to occur eventually, that state may decide it would rather fight in the present than later, when it will be relatively weaker or disadvantaged.[20]

Past research has found that anticipatory attacks are uncommon, in part because of the domestic and international blowback associated with being seen as the aggressor. Still, such motives have been major drivers of consequential interstate wars, including World War I, China's intervention in the Korean War, and the 1967 Arab-Israeli War.[21]

---

[18] For a discussion of how elevated threat perceptions can lead to exaggerated views of a rival's hostility and intentions, see Jervis, 1976.

[19] This term comes from past RAND research (Karl P. Mueller, Jasen J. Castillo, Forrest E. Morgan, Negeen Pegahi, and Brian Rosen, *Striking First: Preemptive and Preventive Attack in U.S. National Security Policy,* RAND Corporation, MG-403-AF, 2006).

[20] Jack S. Levy, "Preventive War: Concept and Propositions," *International Interactions,* Vol. 37, No. 1, 2011; Mueller et al., 2006.

[21] Scholars debate which of these are preemptive versus preventive, but these are all widely seen as anticipatory wars (Dan Reiter, "Exploding the Powder Keg Myth: Preemptive Wars Almost Never Happen," *International Security,* Vol. 20, No. 2, Fall 1995; Stephen Van Evera, *Causes of War: Structures of Power and the Roots of International Conflict,* Cornell University Press, 1999). Some scholars have listed the following as

Although the absolute likelihood of Russia or the United States (and its allies) launching an anticipatory attack is low given the consequences, dynamics in Future 1 could increase this risk compared with the other futures and the status quo antebellum. As discussed previously, Russia sees NATO as committed to defending its own member-states, so it knows that a large-scale anticipatory attack would lead to a full-scale war with a much more powerful alliance. For Russia to launch an anticipatory attack, it would need to believe both that it had something to gain by striking first and that war was almost inevitable.[22] We therefore consider whether the dynamics in Future 1 would make Moscow more likely to come to these two beliefs.

In 2020, a RAND review of Russian military strategy found that Moscow believed that in the event of a war, the United States would use long-range strike systems early to attack Russian leadership, command and control, nuclear, and other military targets. Given its own weakness and limited defenses against such systems, Russia would feel pressure to strike first against these long-range fire systems to degrade U.S. capabilities and use Russian systems before they were destroyed.[23] In Future 1, Russia is weaker than before the war, and U.S. deployment of additional forces in Europe, including intermediate-range missiles, could further exacerbate Moscow's concerns about the vulnerability of key leadership and military targets. Therefore, first strike pressures would be higher than before the war. Still, Russia is unlikely to act on these first strike pressures unless conflict appeared to be inevitable.

In Future 1, there is a greater risk—but not a high likelihood—that Russia would develop such a view. Past RAND research identified scenarios to illustrate how military activities like those envisioned in Future 1 increase

---

additional cases of preventive wars since 1816: the Austro-Prussian War, the Franco-Prussian War, World War II, and the 1956 Suez Crisis (Dale C. Copeland, *The Origins of Major War*, Cornell University Press, 2000; Jack S. Levy and Joseph R. Gochal, "Democracy and Preventive War: Israel and the 1956 Sinai Campaign," *Security Studies*, Vol. 11, No. 2, Autumn 2001; Randall L. Schweller, "Domestic Structure and Preventive War: Are Democracies More Pacific?" *World Politics*, Vol. 44, No. 2, January 1992).

[22] On the importance of inevitability and gains from striking first in motivating preemptive attacks, see Mueller et al., 2006.

[23] Charap et al., 2020, pp. 30–35.

the risk that an action by NATO or Russia could be misperceived as a step toward war, inadvertently creating a sense of inevitability.[24] For example, NATO countries could see a large-scale Russian snap exercise in Belarus as a cover for moving forces in place to attack Lithuania or Latvia. Moscow, in turn, might see the movement of U.S. and other allies' ground forces into the Baltic states as a prelude to intervention in Belarus. To prevent such an outcome, Russia might conduct a limited attack on forces that appear to be involved in such an operation. The NATO response could, in turn, lead to a wider war. In short, with political tensions running high, increased U.S. deployments of long-range strike to Europe, and greater Russian weakness in Future 1, the chance of Moscow launching an anticipatory war in a scenario like this one is higher than before the war, even if it is not likely in absolute terms.

While it is implausible that NATO would launch an unprovoked war of aggression against Russia, it is possible that countries along its eastern flank could misinterpret Russian behavior, mistaking an exercise for prelude to war, for example, and immediately escalate to ensure U.S. involvement. Past RAND research has found that some NATO allies' doctrines call for such early escalation to avoid providing Russia the opportunity to exploit ambiguity.[25]

In addition to these more direct pathways, conflict recurrence in Ukraine would reopen another set of pathways to a Russia-NATO conflict. Previous RAND research has detailed why the risk of such a war has been elevated during the current Russia-Ukraine war. For example, if Russia faced the prospect of defeat, it might take the risk of limited strikes on NATO member-states to disrupt supply lines to Ukraine. Or, if Russia saw military activities in NATO countries as indications that allies were about to enter the war, it could strike that country preemptively.[26] A similar logic would apply if there were another full-scale Russia-Ukraine war, assuming NATO allies once again supported Ukraine. Moreover, although the United States and its allies stayed out of the current war, Russian actions could

---

[24] Charap et al., 2020, pp. 40–41.

[25] Charap et al., 2020.

[26] Frederick et al., 2022.

provoke some NATO member-states to defend Ukraine in a second conflict. Renewed conflict in a country that borders several NATO allies and is the recipient of significant Western aid would once again elevate risks of a clash between Russia and NATO member-states compared with the period before February 2022 or after the signing of the ceasefire. The risk of Russia-Ukraine conflict recurrence is high in this future (as detailed in a following section), and the United States is likely to support Ukraine if war does recur. Therefore, the risk of escalation to a NATO-Russia war is also elevated.

Future 2. The likelihood NATO-Russia conflict due to misperception about intentions is lower in Future 2 than in Future 1 because of the lower level of political and military tensions.

Some commentators in the United States might predict that a U.S. drawdown in Europe and other elements of the less hardline approach would embolden Russia to use force again against Ukraine, other states in the region, or even NATO member-states. Although Russia's imperialist ambitions endure in the postwar period in Future 2, recent RAND analysis has found that less hardline U.S. approaches in peacetime have not made the Kremlin more likely to act on such ambitions in the past. For example, there is no evidence that Moscow saw U.S. policies during the U.S.-Soviet détente or the U.S.-Russia reset as signals of waning U.S. resolve.[27] On the whole, the risk of direct conflict as a result of NATO-Russia competition is lower than in Future 1. Still, tensions are higher than before the war, so the risk does not return to pre-war levels.

If war recurs in Ukraine, there would be an elevated prospect of a clash between Russia and NATO member-states, as in Future 1. However, there are fewer pathways to renewed conflict in Ukraine than in Future 1, as detailed in a later section.

Future 3. As in Future 1, U.S.-Russia political and military tensions are running high. However, in this future, a weaker Russia is unable devote as many resources to prepare for a high-end conventional conflict with NATO. This could limit the intensity of the military buildup on both sides, reducing the risk of a conventional conflict brought about by misperception or inadvertent escalation compared with Future 1. The risk of conflict in Ukraine,

---

[27] Priebe, Frederick, Evans, et al., 2023.

while still elevated, is lower than in Future 1 or 2 (as detailed in a later section). Therefore, the risk of a NATO-Russia resulting from such a conflict escalating is also lower.

Future 4. Overall political-military tensions between Russia and NATO are lowest in this future. Moreover, with fewer forces and military activities taking place along their shared borders, NATO and Russian forces are less likely to misperceive military activities as steps toward war. There is also a lower risk of a Russia-Ukraine war, a conflict that would carry some risk of escalating to a NATO-Russia war. While the risk of both contingencies is lower than in the other futures, it is higher than it was before the war itself; the tensions created by the original conflict will be felt in some way even in this future.

Risk of U.S.-Russia Nuclear Conflict

The overall risk of nuclear use in a crisis between the United States and Russia is a function of a wide variety of factors. There has been extensive research on the causes of past nuclear crises between Moscow and Washington, such as the Cuban Missile Crisis, as well as on both sides' perceptions of the risk of nuclear use more generally.[28] This research finds that both sides' confidence in their capacities to retaliate after a counterforce first strike creates *crisis stability,* or a situation in which neither state has an incentive to use nuclear weapons first because both are confident in their assured retaliation capability. Such confidence can be undermined when a state's nuclear delivery systems or nuclear command and control nodes become more vulnerable to a first strike. For example, the 1980s Euromissile crisis occurred over Soviet concerns that the United States had the capability to promptly strike nuclear command and control nodes in a so-called decapitation strike. In such cases, the vulnerable side is incentivized to strike first in a crisis to avoid being preempted—what is called *use-them-or-lose-them* concerns. Conversely, mutual vulnerability diminishes incen-

---

[28] See, for example, Charap et al., 2022; Dean A. Wilkening, "Strategic Stability Between the United States and Russia," in David Ochmanek and Michael Sulmeyer, eds., *Challenges in U.S. National Security Policy: A Festschrift Honoring Edward L. (Ted) Warner,* RAND Corporation, CP-765-RAS, 2014; and Thomas C. Schelling and Morton H. Halperin, *Strategy and Arms Control,* Pergamon-Brassey's, 1985.

tives to use strategic nuclear weapons first in a crisis because preemption is both futile—given the consequences from retaliation—and unnecessary because of confidence in that retaliatory capability. As discussed previously, the United States would face many challenges in achieving nuclear primacy over Russia and actually overcoming Russia's assured retaliation capabilities. But, even changes in the *perceptions* of the survivability of second strike nuclear capabilities can be destabilizing as leaders act on their newfound *beliefs* that there is an advantage to striking first.

The literature also suggests that transparency can promote crisis stability. Although many aspects of nuclear programs are shrouded in secrecy, Moscow and Washington have found that sharing select information and providing mechanisms for verifying that information can reduce the risk of misperception about each other's capabilities or intentions.[29] For example, verifiable information about warhead numbers can help both sides feel more confident that they have sufficient warheads of their own to engage in a retaliatory strike. Transparency about operations involving nuclear forces can also reduce the risk of misperception.

In the past, U.S. and Russian (or Soviet) leaders have seen arms control as a way to promote crisis stability. For example, limits on strategic warheads and BMD systems sought to reinforce confidence in both sides about their assured retaliation capabilities. Moscow and Washington agreed to the INF treaty in part to give leaders longer decision timelines and reinforce Moscow's confidence in its ability to retaliate. The START treaty and its successor, the NST, have extensive inspection, notification, and data exchange regimes to reduce the likelihood of misperception or miscalculation.

To be clear, crisis stability does not rule out nuclear use. But the absence of crisis stability makes some pathways to nuclear use more likely. Therefore, for each future, we discuss how postwar dynamics affect crisis stability.

Future 1. The risk of nuclear use during the postwar decade is elevated compared with the status quo ante bellum. Both the United States and Russia

---

[29] Vladimir Dvorkin, "Preserving Strategic Stability Amid US-Russian Confrontation," Carnegie Moscow Center, February 2019, p. 7; Linton F. Brooks, "The End of Arms Control?" *Daedalus*, Vol. 149, No. 2, Spring 2020, pp. 91, 108–110. For a concrete example of how transparency in the deployment of SSBNs could be implemented with the goal of increasing strategic stability, see Charap et al., 2022, pp. 54–56.

are building up and deploying new capabilities, and Moscow is threatening to renew nuclear testing. These developments and the collapse of bilateral arms control decrease crisis stability in a number of ways.

First, the deployment of intermediate range missiles to Europe has added to the potential for instability. Ground-based intermediate range systems deployed to NATO Europe could threaten Russia's nuclear command and control capabilities, thus adding to preemption pressure in a crisis.

Second, in the midst of an intense nuclear arms race without information-sharing and verification regimes, there would be greater uncertainty about each side's capabilities. This uncertainty could lead Russia to be more concerned about its assured retaliation capability.

Finally, the end of the NST and strategic dialogue would also mean less transparency about nuclear activities, increasing the chance of catastrophic misunderstanding or miscalculation. For example, under the NST, an exercise involving ICBM test launches would be reported to the other party. Without such notifications, these tests could be misinterpreted as preparation for an attack. Absent arms control, the two strategic communities have little connectivity that could be used to address such a crisis. With political and military tensions high in this future, misinterpretation could lead to nuclear signaling potentially creating a spiral and increasing the chance of preemptive action.

While none of these dynamics need automatically produce a strategic exchange, the guardrails to prevent one would erode significantly in Future 1. Therefore, as with conventional war, a U.S.-Russia nuclear exchange is a low-probability event, but one that is more likely in this future than it was before the Russia-Ukraine war.

Future 2. The risk of nuclear use is lower in Future 2 compared with Future 1 because of lower political tensions and the return to some degree of U.S.-Russia arms control through coordinated unilateral commitments to NST ceilings and a more restrained U.S. nuclear policy. The United States faces relatively fewer prospects of unintended escalation, crisis instability, and misunderstanding with Russia, which still possesses the world's largest nuclear arsenal. That said, these risks are higher than in the pre-war period because there are no legally binding arms control treaties with all the stabilizing measures—such as notifications, on-site verification, and data exchange—that they entail.

Future 3. Growing Russian insecurity from a position of conventional weakness means that the risk of nuclear use is higher than in both the previous futures. All the risks noted in Future 1 are present here (e.g., mutual buildups, no arms control). But in that future, Moscow had more conventional capabilities and did not need to rely heavily on nuclear weapons to deter its adversaries. Here, it does. This is a dynamic similar to the Cold War, when NATO's perceived relative conventional weakness to the Warsaw Pact led it to rely more on nuclear weapons in its war planning. Russia did the same in the 1990s at the low point in its conventional power, but political relations were better at the time and the risk of crisis thus much lower. Moscow's greater reliance on nuclear weapons for deterrence increases the likelihood of their use in a crisis or conflict.

Future 4. Even though Russia is weak in this future, as it is in Future 3, a less hardline U.S. strategy here means that the Kremlin is less insecure so has less incentive to engage in its destabilizing nuclear saber-rattling. Strategic stability is stronger here than in any of the other futures because broader political tensions are lower, closer to the status quo antebellum. The resumption of U.S.-Russia bilateral arms control further reduces the risk of nuclear use as well, compared with Futures 1 and 3.

Risk of a Conventional Conflict with China

The risk of conventional conflict with China will be driven primarily by developments beyond the scope of this study, such as changes in China's intentions, U.S. strategy in the Indo-Pacific region, and China's perceptions of U.S. military activities. We therefore cannot make assessments about how events in our futures would affect U.S.-China conflict risks.

It is noteworthy that U.S. policymakers have frequently drawn a connection between U.S. support to Ukraine during the current war and the risk of conflict with China over Taiwan: namely, that successfully denying Russia its goals in Ukraine will make China less likely to invade Taiwan.[30] But research on states' perceptions of their rivals' past crisis behavior finds

---

[30] See, for example, Biden's speech explaining the importance of U.S. aid to Ukraine in deterring rivals such as China; "Full Transcript: Biden's Speech on Israel-Hamas and Russia-Ukraine Wars," *New York Times*, October 19, 2023.

that states tend to give much more weight to a rival's policies in their own bilateral interactions than in crises involving third states.[31] In other words, China is not likely to weigh U.S. policies toward Russia during the current crisis heavily when considering whether the United States would fight to defend Taiwan.

Although there is no direct research on how *peacetime* behavior (such as that examined in the futures) toward one state affects other states' perceptions of U.S. willingness to fight, logically, it is likely to have even less impact on Chinese perceptions. Therefore, we see no grounds for assuming that U.S. strategy toward Russia will have a significant impact on the likelihood of U.S.-China conventional conflict. We do not include it in Figure 5.2 as a result.

Risk of U.S.-China Nuclear Conflict

The overall risk of U.S.-China nuclear conflict will be determined by many factors, most of which are unrelated to the dynamics in our futures.[32] However, the extent, pace, and scope of U.S. nuclear modernization and the deployment of related strategic capabilities (e.g., BMD) in the four futures would be relevant, in so far as these developments affect Beijing's confidence in its retaliatory capacity. The lack of such confidence could drive crisis instability. In the past, China has seen the development of U.S. BMD and counterforce capabilities (conventional and nuclear) as threats to its assured retaliation capability. In response, China has expanded its nuclear arsenal and enhanced the survivability of its systems. China also adopted some ambiguity about its no-first-use nuclear doctrine.[33] U.S.-Russia arms control will also affect U.S.-China strategic stability. Arms control agreements that put upper ceilings on U.S. (and Russian) nuclear arsenals provide

---

[31] For an overview of the extensive literature and most applicable analysis on the topic, see Alex Weisiger and Keren Yarhi-Milo, "Revisiting Reputation: How Past Actions Matter in International Politics," *International Organization*, Vol. 69, No. 2, Spring 2015.

[32] For a discussion of some of these other factors, see Fiona S. Cunningham and M. Taylor Fravel, "Dangerous Confidence? Chinese Views on Nuclear Escalation," *International Security*, Vol. 44, No. 2, Fall 2019; and Caitlin Talmadge, "Would China Go Nuclear? Assessing the Risk of Chinese Nuclear Escalation in a Conventional War with the United States," *International Security*, Vol. 41, No. 4, Spring 2017.

[33] Cunningham and Fravel, 2015.

important baselines for Chinese nuclear planners. Without those ceilings on U.S. forces, Chinese planners could make worst-case projections about the vulnerability of their retaliatory capability.

Future 1. In Future 1, the collapse of U.S.-Russia arms control and hardline U.S. nuclear policy lead to the expansion and further technological development of systems that China could find threatening. As discussed previously, it would be difficult for the United States actually to undermine China's second strike capability. But given an intense arms race and significant uncertainty, Beijing could see such an outcome as plausible over time. In response, China could focus on enhancing survivability, including by expanding its arsenal. It could also move further away from or even entirely abandon its no-first-use doctrine to deter the United States. Such a development would increase the relative risk of U.S.-China nuclear conflict, even if the risk of such an outcome is not high in absolute terms.

Future 2. The dynamics in Future 2—a more restrained U.S. nuclear policy and a return to modest U.S.-Russia arms control—are likely to prove more stabilizing than those in Future 1. A status quo U.S. BMD program and unchanged nuclear modernization plan would create fewer first strike concerns than in Future 1.

Future 3. Beijing's responses to U.S. capability development and abandonment of U.S.-Russia arms control create similar dynamics as in Future 1, increasing the risk of a U.S.-China nuclear conflict relative to Futures 2 and 4 and to the status quo antebellum.

Future 4. In Future 4, the stabilizing effects of more-restrained U.S. nuclear policy is even stronger than in Future 2 due to more-robust U.S.-Russia arms control that creates greater certainty about U.S. capabilities and therefore increases Beijing's confidence in its ability to retaliate.

Strength of the U.S. Economy

In this section, we consider how global economic fragmentation and direct economic fallout from the war affect U.S. prosperity in each future. As of late 2023, there is already movement toward global economic fragmentation as a result of the Russia-Ukraine war. Western countries have imposed sanctions on Russia in retaliation for the invasion. Russia, China, and some other states have taken steps toward reducing their reliance on the West by, for example, diversifying their currency reserves, conducting transactions in currencies other than the U.S. dollar or Euro, and developing alternative trade and financial arrangements.[34] These steps have been aimed, at least in part, at reducing vulnerability to possible future Western sanctions or, in Russia's case, reacting to those already in place.

Studies have shown that economic fragmentation reduces U.S. economic growth.[35] When trade, investment, and other ties are increasingly driven by security concerns, not just economic efficiency considerations, international exchange becomes less profitable, which undermines growth. Even though the U.S. dollar would likely remain the dominant global currency in the four futures, as more transactions take place in other currencies and U.S. rivals and many other states continue to diversify their reserves away from U.S. treasury bonds, the dollar would somewhat weaken relative to other currencies and U.S. borrowing costs would increase.[36]

In all the futures, we assume that global economic fragmentation continues during and after the war. But the speed and extent of the fragmentation differs, and thus the effects on the U.S. economy are different.

In addition to accelerating fragmentation, the war and related dynamics also have also been a drag on the European economy, stemming from the disruption of trade with Russia, direct budgetary outlays for aiding Ukraine and hosting refugees, and general uncertainty about the future. Research suggests that economic conditions in Europe modestly affect the U.S. economy.[37] Slower growth in European economies lowers demand for U.S. goods and services and reduces possible profits from U.S. investment in Europe. Because Europe (i.e., the EU and the UK) is a key U.S. trade and investment partner, slowdowns there brought on by the disruptions stemming from the Russia-Ukraine war or from expectations of another one will have negative

---

[34] Marc Jones, "JPMorgan Flags Some Signs of Emerging De-Dollarisation," Reuters, June 5, 2023.

[35] Felbermayr, Mahlkow, and Sandkamp, 2023.

[36] The effects of a weakening dollar on U.S. growth are difficult to predict. However, lower demand for U.S. treasury bonds would increase borrowing costs.

[37] Ozge Akinci and Paolo Pesenti, "Do Economic Crises in Europe Affect the U.S.? Some Lessons from the Past Three Decades," *Liberty Street Economics*, May 31, 2023.

consequences for the U.S. economy. As with the pace and extent of economic fragmentation, European economic challenges vary across the four futures.

It should be noted that the United States has a large and diverse economy and trades with many economic partners globally. This enables the United States to adapt to economic challenges better than other states and mitigate, but not eliminate, the effects of dynamics similar to those we discuss in this section. Therefore, the effects we discuss here are likely to be only modestly negative compared with pre-war trends rather than major drags on the U.S. economy. Figure 5.3 shows a summary of our analysis.

Future 1. The intensity of great power competition in Future 1 accelerates the global trend toward economic fragmentation, which, in turn, has a modestly negative impact on U.S. growth prospects. In this future, the long war slows European growth.[38] European countries' aid to Ukraine diverts funds from domestic investments and creates budgetary pressures. In the postwar period, the high risk (detailed in a later section) of another Russia-Ukraine war creates uncertainty and supply chain disruptions, inhibiting investment.[39]

Future 2. As in Future 1, the long war in Ukraine weakens European economies. But the chance of another war is somewhat lower than in Future 1 (as detailed in the following section), decreasing uncertainty around economic investments in Europe and the ripple effects for the U.S. economy. In the postwar period, global economic fragmentation that began during the war continues because many Western sanctions on Russia and China remain in place and both rivals make efforts to limit dependence on the West. This fragmentation drags on U.S. growth compared with the pre-war trajectory. However, the intensity of political and military competition

---

[38] For an assessment of effect of the war on Europe's economy already and a prediction that the economic effects of the war will increase, see Jonas Bruhin, Rolf Scheufele, and Yannic Stucki, "The Economic Impact of Russia's Invasion of Ukraine on European Countries—a SVAR Approach," SSRN Working Paper No. 04-2024, September 22, 2023. For models suggesting negative effects on European economies from economic fragmentation, see Felbermayr, Mahlkow, and Sandkamp, 2023.

[39] For a more detailed discussion of how instability affects investment, trade, and growth, see Bryan Rooney, Grant Johnson, Tobias Sytsma, and Miranda Priebe, *Does the U.S. Economy Benefit from U.S. Alliances and Forward Military Presence?* RAND Corporation, RR-A739-5, 2022.

is lower, so the pace of economic fragmentation is slower than in Future 1. The resulting impact on U.S. growth is less negative.

Future 3. The negative economic consequences from dynamics in Future 3 are less severe than those in Future 1. Economic fragmentation is less pronounced than in Future 1 because the West does not sanction China during the war. The shorter war and lower risk of conflict recurrence in Ukraine (detailed in a later section) make European economies stronger than in Future 1.

The comparison with Future 2 is more uncertain. The shorter war and lower risk of conflict recurrence in Ukraine are better for growth in Europe than in Future 2. While there is less economic fragmentation during the war in Future 3, there is more of it in the postwar period because of increased tensions with Russia and China. We have no empirical basis to assess whether the drag on growth would be more significant in Future 3 compared with Future 2. Therefore, we treat it as equal in both futures in our summary figure (Figure 5.3).

Future 4. In this future, Europe's economic recovery—enabled by a shorter war and growing sense that peace will prevail—is comparatively more conducive to U.S. economic growth as trade ties recover and private sector actors pursue profitable investments in Europe. Other trends—such as the slower pace of economic decoupling in this future—are also modestly more favorable for U.S. economic growth than in other futures. Overall, this future has the best implications for U.S. growth outlook among the four.

FIGURE 5.3

How Dynamics in Each Future Affect the U.S. Economy Relative to Pre-War Trends

	Future 1: Pervasive Instability	Future 2: Localized Instability	Future 3: Cold War 2.0	Future 4: Cold Peace
Strength of the U.S. economy	✕✕✕✕	✕✕✕	✕✕✕	✕

NOTE: Darker red and more crosses represent worse outcomes compared to pre-war trends. The absolute size of the economic effects would likely be modest across all four futures. See the text for assumptions and uncertainties associated with these rough assessments.

Ukraine's Security and Prosperity

In this section, we consider Ukraine's security and prosperity in the postwar decade. To do so, we examine three variables in each future: Ukraine's ability to defend itself in the event of another Russian attack, the likelihood of another Russia-Ukraine war, and the state of Ukraine's economy and democracy (Figure 5.4).

Ukraine's ability to defend the territory that it controls at the end of the war depends on the local balance of power and Kyiv's approach to shaping the UAF and its doctrine over the postwar decade. Russia is a major power with multiple security concerns, so it is unlikely to focus all its defense spending on preparations for another war in Ukraine or bring all its military capability to bear in that event. In the current war in Ukraine, for example, Russia has held some capabilities in reserve in the event of a war with NATO.[40] Therefore, we consider how Russia might prioritize Ukraine in its overall force posture in each future.

We assume that Kyiv would focus its postwar rearmament entirely on preparing for the prospect of another war with Russia. In assessing Ukraine's defenses, we consider the posture Kyiv adopts, the nature of the

FIGURE 5.4
How Dynamics in the Futures Affect Ukraine's Security and Prosperity

	Future 1: Pervasive Instability	Future 2: Localized Instability	Future 3: Cold War 2.0	Future 4: Cold Peace
Ukraine's ability to defend itself	✗✗✗		✓✓✓	✓✓✓✓
Risk of conflict recurrence	✗✗✗✗	✗✗	✗✗	✗
Ukraine's economy and democracy	✗✗✗✗	✗✗✗	✗✗	✗

NOTE: We compare the futures with one another, ranking them from most favorable (dark green text and more checkmarks) for the United States to neutral (blank gray boxes) to least favorable (dark red text and more crosses). See the text for assumptions and uncertainties associated with these rough assessments.

---

[40] "The Curious Case of Russia's Missing Air Force," *The Economist*, March 8, 2022.

support it gets from third parties, and the resources it can spend on defense. (The United States provides the same level of resources in all four futures, but directs it toward different ends.) We assume that given the same level of resources devoted to the military, Ukraine is more effective at defending territory it already holds using a porcupine strategy rather than investing in an offensive maneuver–capable force. In assessing Ukraine's ability to go on the offense, we also consider available resources and posture.

These assessments are subject to the same challenges of deep uncertainty we faced in assessing the distribution between major powers. In the following paragraphs, we make explicit the assumptions we used to make a net assessment.

Future 1. Despite ongoing economic sanctions, Russia is in a relatively better position than Ukraine to rearm and recover economically given that its infrastructure and military industry were not nearly as affected by the war. Beijing provided wartime support, and postwar defense cooperation also enables Russia's recovery. At the same time, Ukraine is largely dependent on U.S. support because its own economy is weak and other allies are not contributing as much as expected to its recovery due to concerns about Kyiv's intentions to restart hostilities.

In this future, the higher risk of a NATO-Russia conflict and nuclear arms race with the United States would require more resources. The effect on the local balance of power with Ukraine would depend on how many resources Russia diverts toward capabilities unique to the high-end fight or nuclear conflict, the strength of Russia's economy, and Moscow's ability to increase defense spending to pursue multiple priorities.

The impact of these dynamics on the local balance of power is uncertain. To make a judgment, we assume that an imperialist Russia would spend more on defense to pursue its goals in Ukraine and that its economy would enable it to do so. There is some recent evidence to suggest that it could do so, particularly if oil prices are high.[41] If Russia's ability to devote resources to preparing for an attack on Ukraine outpaces Ukraine's ability to spend on defense, the distribution of power would shift in Russia's

---

[41] Patricia Cohen, "Russia's Economy Is Increasingly Structured Around Its War in Ukraine," *New York Times*, October 9, 2023, 2023; Janis Kluge, "The West Shouldn't Underestimate Russia's Resilience," *Moscow Times*, September 15, 2023.

favor. This dynamic would be particularly problematic in Future 1, in which Ukrainian posture is not optimized for defense. In such a situation, Kyiv would struggle to defend the territory it already controls if conflict recurs. Although Ukraine has capabilities to go on the offensive in Future 1 (thanks to U.S. support), it would struggle to retake territory against an increasingly capable Russia.

Future 2. There are multiple differences between Futures 1 and 2 relevant to the local distribution of power. Adopting a porcupine strategy optimized for defense should allow Ukraine to better defend the territory it already controls given the same level of resources. Moreover, allies provide more resources to Kyiv than in Future 1 because they are more comfortable with Ukraine's military posture.

However, postwar U.S.-Russia competition is less intense than in Future 1, so Russia does not need to devote as many resources to preparing for a high-end fight with NATO or a nuclear buildup. This frees up Russian resources to focus on a Ukraine contingency.

On net, the local balance would likely be more favorable to Ukraine in this future than in Future 1 because of the defense-dominant nature of the current Russia-Ukraine war as of this writing. Most of both sides' attempted ground offensives have failed, and well-constructed defenses have proven extremely effective. Therefore, we assume that Ukraine's adoption of the porcupine strategy leaves it in a better position than in Future 1, even though Russia likely has more resources if it decides to attack.

Future 3. Ukraine's ability to defend itself is better than in Future 1. The shorter war means Ukraine has faced fewer combat losses and its economy and infrastructure are less damaged. Moreover, allies are (because of better economic circumstances) more able to help Ukraine rearm and more willing to do so because they are reassured by its improved democratic credentials and adherence to the ceasefire. Finally, Ukraine's economic growth means it is developing a stronger basis to sustain its own defense spending in the long term and becoming less reliant on the United States and its allies compared with Future 1. This should translate into better abilities to both defend itself and go on the offensive than in Future 1.

The comparison between Futures 2 and 3 requires accounting for most of the same dynamics. There is however, one important difference: Without U.S. encouragement, Ukraine builds a force capable of offensive maneuver rather than one optimized for defense and resiliency. But with better starting conditions and more postwar resources, Ukraine would likely be more able to defend the territory it already controls in Future 3 than in Future 2.

Future 4. Among the four futures, Ukraine is best able to defend the territory it controls in Future 4. Ukraine has the most resources for defense in this future—from other NATO allies and as a result of its own growing economy—to invest in its own defense. Investing these greater resources in a porcupine strategy means Ukraine is well situated to defend itself against Russia.

Risk of Conflict Recurrence

We consider how dynamics in each future affect the likelihood of three pathways to another Russia-Ukraine conflict in the postwar period:

- intentional decision to attack due to postwar gains in relative power
- preventive conflict due to adverse shifts in the distribution of power
- escalation along the LoC.

There may be other potential pathways to conflict recurrence as well. We focus on these three because they are prominent in the literature on interstate conflict recurrence and because they can be directly linked to the postwar dynamics we discuss in the futures.[42] We assume that the parties rationally respond to postwar trends as they see them. In other words, Russia and Ukraine would, in light of postwar dynamics, assess costs, risks, and prospects for success before launching another conflict.[43]

As we detail in a later section, past research has found that postwar changes in the distribution of power have often been the cause of conflict recurrence. The party that recovers more quickly after the war may be more

---

[42] We do not, for example, consider pathways to war that emerge out of domestic political developments or one side launching a war without weighing the costs and benefits. While such pathways to war are possible, the risk of such an outcome is not clearly tied to the dynamics in each future.

[43] Our framework is not, however, strictly *rationalist* as political scientists define the term. For example, as we discuss in the following sections, we consider the possibility that the parties can view the same information and come to different conclusions about its meaning.

likely to intentionally attack to try to make gains. By contrast, preventative conflicts emerge when the party in relative declines worries it needs to act before trends further move against it. Escalation along the LoC can also lead to conflict recurrence because of mistrust, miscalculation, or misunderstanding, as well as difficulties making ceasefires stick. Figure 5.5 summarizes our assessment of the likelihood of these different pathways to conflict in the four futures.

Risk of Conflict Because of Perceptions of Strength

If the two sides rearm at a similar rate after the war, then the distribution of power is stable. In such situations, neither party can be confident that more fighting will deliver a better outcome than the status quo at the end of the war. Therefore, neither side has an incentive to restart the conflict. However, when one side recovers more quickly, it may be more likely to restart the conflict to try to make additional gains.[44] Many factors affect states' decisions to go to war, and conflicts can sometimes be averted through negotiations, so shifts in the distribution of power are not certain to lead to conflict. Still, such situations raise the risk of conflict recurrence.

FIGURE 5.5
Risk of Pathways to Conflict Recurrence Across Futures

	Future 1: Pervasive Instability	Future 2: Localized Instability	Future 3: Cold War 2.0	Future 4: Cold Peace
Risk of conflict due to perceptions of strength	✕✕✕✕		✕✕	✕
Risk of preventive conflict	✕✕✕✕	✕✕	✕✕✕	✕
Risk of escalation along the line of contact	✕✕✕✕	✕✕✕✕	✕	✕

NOTE: We compare the futures with one another, ranking them from most favorable (dark green text and more checkmarks) for the United States to neutral (blank gray boxes) to least favorable (dark red text and more crosses). See the text for assumptions and uncertainties associated with these rough assessments.

---

[44] Suzanne Werner, "The Precarious Nature of Peace: Resolving the Issues, Enforcing the Settlement, and Renegotiating the Terms," *American Journal of Political Science*, Vol. 43, No. 3, July 1999, pp. 918–919.

For each future, we consider the likelihood that Kyiv or Moscow intentionally starts a conflict, believing that it is in a better position to make territorial gains than it was when the war ended. We make these assessments based on which side's military recovers more quickly than the other in the postwar period and whether that state has the motive to restart the conflict and what restraints to conflict initiation it may face.

Future 1. As discussed previously, the military balance favors Russia in this future. Russia therefore could become confident that another war would allow it to achieve its imperialistic goals. Moreover, the forces that might restrain Moscow from such aggression are limited. The weak ceasefire stopped the fighting, but it did not provide Russia other significant benefits to keeping the peace. There is less left to lose for Russia when it comes to diplomatic consequences of another war: Moscow's friends will remain its friends, the neutrals will stay neutral, and the rest are enemies already. Russia does, of course, still have more to lose militarily from another war in Ukraine, a factor which could restrain its behavior. Further aggression is thus not inevitable. But the risks are elevated. An isolated Russia has fewer inhibitions on escalation, and Russia's imperialist drive also leads to demands to "finish the job" in Ukraine.

Future 2. The local distribution of power in this future is stable, so it is unlikely that either side will attack out of the conviction that gains through further hostilities are possible.

Futures 3 and 4. Ukraine, rather than Russia, recovers more quickly. In these futures, an economic development–oriented Kyiv believes that another war would be very costly, even if some territory might be gained, so eventual reunification through peaceful means is a better course. Therefore, Kyiv is not as likely to act on its advantages and start a war to liberate more territory as it is in Futures 1 and 2.

Still, intentions can change, so the chance of conflict along this pathway is not zero. Domestic developments in Ukraine, could, for example, bring to power nationalist leaders who seek to resume fighting. Therefore, the conflict risk is lower in Future 4, when Ukraine's posture is optimized for defense and less suited to going on the offense, than in Future 3.

Risk of Preventive Conflict

Simplified conflict models assume that changes in the distribution of power are objective facts that are clear to both rivals. Given this assumption, only one side—the state facing relative decline—should have a preventive motivation to use force. However, in practice, projections about the future distribution are uncertain. In this context, states could come to different conclusions.[45] Therefore, we consider the possibility that both sides could see themselves in relative decline and develop preventive motivations.

Future 1. With Russia recovering more quickly than Ukraine, Kyiv faces the prospect of an adverse shift in the distribution of power. Although the United States is pushing for greater integration with NATO, Kyiv is unlikely to feel confident in eventual membership given the lack of consensus among allies. Therefore, the prospect of future membership may not factor into Ukraine's assessment of the future distribution of power. At the same time, Ukraine has motives to attack. The government is determined to liberate Russia-occupied territory. Moreover, an imperialist Russia seems likely to attack at some point, so Ukraine has incentives to fight before its relative power wanes. And Ukraine's development of an offensive maneuver-capable force means that it has capabilities to attack. These dynamics do not make a Ukraine-initiated preventive war inevitable. Ukraine's relative weakness and the prospect of wartime losses could restrain Ukraine from acting on preventive motives. But the risk of Ukraine restarting the war, believing fighting sooner is better than doing so later, is elevated.

Russia could also have preventive motivations. Most importantly, Moscow may see developments surrounding Ukraine's integration with NATO differently than Kyiv. In 2023, Moscow saw Finland quickly move from being deeply integrated with—but formally outside—NATO to gaining full membership. Russian elites tend to assume that allies will resist U.S. preferences only in extremis, so even division on the issue will not necessarily reassure those elites if Washington is pushing for Ukraine's membership. Therefore, Moscow might renew the war to make Ukraine an unattractive candidate if it thinks membership is becoming a foregone conclusion.

---

[45] For the idea that states can come to differing views about the distribution of power, see Jonathan Kirshner, "Rationalist Explanations for War?," *Security Studies*, Vol. 10, No. 1, Autumn 2000.

Finally, Russia may have another motive to attack that is closely related to preventive logic.[46] This logic, sometimes referred to as "mowing the grass," aims to use limited force to reduce a rival's capabilities to deter it from launching a wider war or, failing that, making it less capable. The approach is most closely associated with Israel's recurrent limited strikes on such groups as Hamas, conducted over the years prior to the October 7, 2023, terror attacks.[47]

In Future 1, Russia may conduct periodic limited strikes on military targets, especially the advanced capabilities provided by the West, in the hopes that it can attrit Ukraine's capabilities to liberate occupied territory. A limited conflict could escalate to war if Ukraine responds forcefully to Russian strikes. In the extreme, Russia might decide to launch an all-out war to neutralize the threat posed by a UAF armed with advanced capabilities provided by Washington.

Future 2. The United States does not rhetorically support Ukraine's NATO membership in this future. These words are matched by deeds: The United States does not actually integrate Ukraine's military with NATO. Thus, Russia has less incentive in this future to preventively strike Ukraine in an attempt to foreclose the country's accession. Moreover, the United States and its allies are not providing Ukraine with as much offensive capability, decreasing Russia's incentives to "mow the grass" with limited strikes on military targets.

Ukraine is also unlikely to act according to a preventive logic in Future 2 because the military balance is stable. Furthermore, it does not have an ideal force posture for launching an attack. Certain capabilities could be dual-purposed and used to go on the offense, but overall, its strategy is optimized for defense. Therefore, Ukraine would find it more difficult to act on preventive motivations even if it had such motivations.

Future 3. Ukraine does not have preventive motives in this future. The country's economic recovery and Russia's setbacks give Kyiv the sense that the balance of power will only improve in Kyiv's favor with time. Moreover,

---

[46] Strictly speaking, preventive conflicts begin as a result of an adverse shift in relative power. Here, the stronger state is responding to an absolute gain by a rival.

[47] Efraim Inbar and Eitan Shamir, "'Mowing the Grass': Israel's Strategy for Protracted Intractable Conflict," *Journal of Strategic Studies*, Vol. 37, No. 1, 2014.

Ukraine is focused on economic development and does not see a military solution to the problem. Russia appears less imperialistic and thus less likely to attack.

In this future, Moscow is concerned about both U.S. offensive military assistance to Kyiv and Washington's continued pushing of Ukraine's NATO membership, giving it more preventive motive than in Future 2. But Ukraine's formal neutrality pledge—and its lack of militarism and outward efforts at territorial reconquest—provide fewer incentives for Russia to engage in preventive conflict than in Future 1. Gaining confidence with time that NATO membership for Ukraine is unlikely, a security-focused Russia is less motivated to restart the war to forestall such an outcome. Given Ukraine's restrained policies, Russia has less incentive to engage in a preventive strike on the UAF. Furthermore, compared with the challenges from the United States and NATO in this future, Ukraine is less of an urgent Russian priority.

Future 4. In this future, Moscow is even less likely to act on preventive motivations than it is in Future 3. The United States is not pushing for Ukraine's membership in NATO or providing offensively oriented assistance. Thus, Moscow's security concerns are less pressing than in Futures 1 and 3. Preventive motives are even less pronounced here than in Future 2, since Ukraine shows little interest in starting another war.

Risk of Escalation Along the Line of Contact

This pathway entails an escalation spiral along the LoC. It could begin with Ukrainian sabotage operations or Russian shelling across the line and quickly escalate to renewed war. To assess this risk, we first consider the motives of both sides and the strength of forces that might restrain each side from ceasefire violations. We also consider the nature of the ceasefire.

As noted previously, past research suggests that conflict recurrence is less likely with a robust rather than weak ceasefire. Such ceasefires reduce the likelihood of conflict recurrence through measures that disincentivize using force, provide information to reduce the risk of misperception, and offer processes for addressing possible ceasefire violations.[48] For example, ceasefires that contain physical constraints, such as troop withdrawals,

---

[48] Fortna, 2003, p. 340.

demilitarized buffer zones, and arms control agreements can reduce the likelihood of a successful surprise attack and prevent accidents and misunderstandings from occurring in the first place. The presence of outside monitors who can impartially identify which side violated the ceasefire can raise the costs of reigniting conflict by creating expectations that an aggressor will face international opprobrium. Parties that agree to such monitors send a costly signal about their willingness to abide by the ceasefire. Outside monitors can investigate and mediate incidents, preventing accidental violations of the ceasefire from escalating.[49] Peacekeepers can ensure compliance, address minor issues before they escalate, create a buffer to prevent incidents, and provide a "moral barrier" to resuming hostilities.[50]

Ukraine has a recent history of having a weak ceasefire that demonstrates the pitfalls associated with such documents. The so-called Minsk Agreements, signed in September 2014 and February 2015, had few of the characteristics of robust ceasefires. They were extremely vague and had no effective monitoring or accountability mechanisms. The key security provisions—cessation of hostilities and withdrawal of heavy weapons—were never fully implemented. In part, that stemmed from the lack of agreement on the LoC and nonimplementation of disengagement arrangements and a weak monitoring mission.

Future 1. Tensions along the LoC are likely to be high in this future. Ukraine's desire to keep the hope of liberation alive leads it to engage in sabotage activities and support for insurgent groups in occupied areas. Russia's imperialist drive to subjugate Ukraine could result in more cross-LoC attacks on the UAF and the violent repression of civilians in occupied areas. The two militaries are operating in close proximity, so if one side's behavior is seen as a belligerent act, the other might quickly respond with force. Each side's responses to the other's actions could lead to an escalatory spiral along the LoC. With only a weak ceasefire, there are no mechanisms for dispute resolution and no monitoring or peacekeeping missions to clarify misperceptions.

---

[49] Fortna, 2003, pp. 342–345.

[50] Virginia Page Fortna, "Interstate Peacekeeping: Causal Mechanisms and Empirical Effects," *World Politics*, Vol. 56, No. 4, July 2004b, p. 485.

Given these dynamics, the United States and its European allies might try to put pressure on both sides to abide by the ceasefire. However, as discussed previously, Russia may feel that it has little to lose from other countries' reactions to another war. The forces that might, in theory, restrain Ukraine are also limited in practice. Ukraine's military weakness should encourage caution, but instead, Kyiv's grievances drive it to take action. The societal demand for justice and revenge could fuel strong domestic political pressure for Ukraine's leadership to respond forcefully to Russian ceasefire violations. Ukraine's dependence on the United States could give Washington leverage to restrain Kyiv from raising the risk of conflict or escalating too quickly in response to Russian provocations. However, given the U.S. view of Russian intentions (i.e., inherently aggressive) and the U.S. hardline approach in this future, the United States is unlikely to do so. The lack of a realistic pathway to EU membership and the lower levels of support from European powers gives Brussels less leverage as well. Moreover, Ukraine's offensive posture could give Kyiv hope that it can retake some of its lost territory.

Future 2. The same dynamics as in Future 1 mean that the risk of escalation along the LoC is equally high. The United States encourages Ukraine to respect the ceasefire and adopt a defensive posture in this future, but it refuses to exercise coercive leverage when Kyiv takes assertive actions across the LoC.

Futures 3 and 4. A localized conflict resulting from ceasefire violations is far less likely in these futures than in Futures 1 and 2. The robust ceasefire agreement provides for greater stability on the ground. Furthermore, neither Russia nor Ukraine is inclined in these futures to take offensive action.

Ukraine's Economy and Democracy

Future 1. Economically and politically, Ukraine emerges from the postwar decade in rough shape in Future 1. Already poor before the war and economically decimated by the longer conflict and its knock-on effects, the country does not bounce back in this future. In fact, it continues a downward slide. Ukraine's prioritization of reconquest over economic development make the country less attractive for citizens and investors and alienate its key EU partners, derailing its membership bid.

Politically, Ukraine was already displaying authoritarian tendencies during the war.[51] For example, the 2022 Reporters Without Borders World Press Freedom Index ranked Ukraine 106th out of 180, a decline of nine positions from 2021.[52] The extreme centralization of power that occurred during the long war continues in the postwar period, further eroding Ukraine's democracy.[53]

Future 2. In Future 2, there is modestly more postwar economic recovery than in Future 1 as a result of the lower risk of conflict, but the overall state of the Ukrainian economy is poor. In both futures, authoritarian tendencies compound the economic effects of the war and derail the country's EU membership bid.

Future 3. In Future 3, Ukraine is more prosperous and free (than in Futures 1 and 2) due to the shorter war, the government's focus on recovery and economic development, and the lower risk of conflict recurrence. Equally, the progress on EU integration and the incentives created by the membership process help ensure the consolidation of Ukraine's democracy.

Future 4. In Future 4, Ukraine is the most prosperous and free. The lowest conflict risk encourages the most refugees and investors to return to contribute to the economy. The lower conflict risk and focus on recovery reduce militarism, and the pathway to EU membership encourages democratic reforms.

Minimizing Conflict Risk in Other Non-NATO Former Soviet States

Russia sees itself as a regional leader, and Moscow has repeatedly responded to perceived Western encroachment with coercion or force against states in

---

[51] Timothy Colton, "Ukraine and Russia: War and Political Regimes," *Journal of Democracy*, Vol. 33, No. 4, October 2022.

[52] Reporters Without Borders, "RSF's 2022 World Press Freedom Index: A New Era of Polarisation," May 3, 2022.

[53] Lührmann and Rooney, 2021.

post-Soviet Eurasia.[54] Past RAND research has shown that these interventions have been triggered by a variety of factors, in particular "changes on the ground in post-Soviet Eurasia that create an external threat or the perception of a rapid change in the regional balance or in Russia's status."[55] Such shocks—e.g., revolutions that bring to power pro-Western governments—are not anticipated in the futures. However, this RAND study also indicated that, more broadly, "Moscow has intervened when it perceived regional balances to be shifting away from a status quo that was favorable to Russian interests."[56] Therefore, we assume that the more active the United States is in its efforts to roll back Russian influence in the region, the more likely Russia is to intervene.[57] That said, proactive U.S. policy in the region does not make Russian intervention inevitable or even likely in an absolute sense. But it would, all else being equal, increase that prospect.[58] It should be noted that we do not account for resource constraints affecting the likelihood of conflict, because Russia's military capabilities are so much greater than those of the five states in question: Armenia, Azerbaijan, Belarus, Georgia, and Moldova (Figure 5.6).

Future 1. In this future, the regional contestation is extremely intense. The U.S. goal is to counter Russia's influence wherever it can and engage extensively in the region. Russia's objective is to minimize American influence *and*, given its imperialist motives, have influence over decisionmaking in all regional capitals. These dynamics drive conflictual interactions, leading Moscow to punish close U.S. partners while tying its allies closer. Given the high level of political and military tensions across the range of bilateral interactions, the prospect of a Russian military intervention in the region is significantly higher than it was before the war.

---

[54] For discussion of these coercive efforts before 2022, see Charap, Massicot, et al., 2021, pp. 47–48, 57–66. We exclude the three Baltic states, which are NATO allies and members of the EU, and the Central Asian countries, as noted previously.

[55] Samuel Charap, Edward Geist, Bryan Frederick, John J. Drennan, Nathan Chandler, and Jennifer Kavanagh, *Russia's Military Interventions: Patterns, Drivers, and Signposts,* RAND Corporation, RR-A444-3, 2021, p. xvi.

[56] Charap, Geist, et al., 2021, p. 137.

[57] Charles E. Ziegler, "A Crisis of Diverging Perspectives: U.S.-Russian Relations and the Security Dilemma," *Texas National Security Review,* Vol. 4, No. 1, Winter 2020–2021.

[58] It should be noted that this is an analytical observation, not a policy prescription.

FIGURE 5.6

Risk That Russia Uses Force in Another Former Soviet Non-NATO Country

	Future 1: Pervasive Instability	Future 2: Localized Instability	Future 3: Cold War 2.0	Future 4: Cold Peace
Minimizing conflict risk in other non-NATO former Soviet states	✕✕✕✕	✕✕	✕✕✕	✓

NOTE: Darker red and more crosses represent worse outcomes compared to pre-war trends. See the text for assumptions and uncertainties associated with these rough assessments.

Future 2. Without the ramping up of U.S. regional engagement seen in Future 1, competition in post-Soviet Eurasia is less intense. But imperialistic tendencies are ascendant in Moscow, and all previous norms have been shattered because of the war and the lack of a negotiated order in its aftermath. The risk of a Russian intervention is thus lower than in Future 1, but still higher than before the war.

Future 3. As in Future 1, greater U.S. involvement in former Soviet non-NATO states provokes Russian responses to limit U.S. influence. While Russia's resources are more constrained after the damaging war, it would still have the capacity to, for example, intervene in Belarus if there were domestic unrest. Thus the risk of intervention is higher than in Future 2 due to the more intense regional competition, but less than in Future 1 because of Russia's focus on security concerns over imperialist ambitions.

Future 4. As in Future 2, the United States is relatively restrained about its activities in states along Russia's periphery. Compared with Futures 1 and 3, therefore, Russia has fewer incentives to use force to protect its interests in those countries. Here, the broader détente and waning of imperialist moods in Moscow probably lead to greater stability in the region compared with Future 2 and the status quo antebellum, when contestation was more intensive than the "new normal" of Future 4. Although the likelihood of Russian intervention in the region is lowest in this future, some risk remains. The contest for influence continues to some degree, and the Kremlin will always be concerned about perceived U.S. encirclement.

Comparing the Futures

Comparing Implications Across Futures

Figure 5.7 summarizes the implications for U.S. interests discussed in this chapter. All assessments are relative to pre-war trends—except for Ukraine's security and prosperity, which is compared across the four futures—and thus represent degrees of benefit or harm to U.S. interests. For example, the four futures leave the United States stronger relative to Russia than before the war. The risk of a U.S.-Russia clash and great power nuclear conflict are higher than before the war.

But within these and the other dimensions, outcomes do vary from a U.S. perspective over the postwar decade. While none of the futures are uniformly positive, Futures 2, 3, and 4 are equal to or better for U.S. interests than Future 1 on almost every dimension. The key exception is that the risk of nuclear conflict with Russia is higher in Future 3 than in Future 1. Future 4 is either more advantageous for the United States on every metric or equally so.

While Future 4 is clearly the most advantageous for the United States, and Future 1 clearly the least beneficial, Futures 2 and 3 feature different trade-offs, so assessing them relative to each other would require prioritization of U.S. interests. For example, Future 2 features modestly worse economic outcomes for the United States, while Future 3 has a higher risk of a rare event: nuclear conflict with a major power. Overall assessments of these futures thus depend on normative judgments about the relative importance of these interests.

Comparing Implications Across Postwar Worlds

While we reduce the postwar worlds to a binary for the purposes of our analysis, it is important to understand which particular aspects have the most influence over the dynamics in the postwar period. To do so, we looked for *similarities* across futures that begin with the same starting conditions but feature different U.S. strategies. We focus on the similarities between Futures 1 and 2, but a similar logic applies to a comparison of Futures 3 and 4.

Several elements of the world had enduring effects over the decade: China's support for Russia during the conflict, the duration of the war, the nature of the ceasefire agreement, and the nature of Kyiv's and Moscow's intentions after the war.

Beijing's military support to Moscow helps Russia strengthen its military while the war is ongoing in World A. In both Futures 1 and 2, this contributes to but does not entirely determine differences in the postwar distribution of power. Furthermore, Western sanctions in response to China's policy change contribute to greater economic fragmentation, which drags on the U.S. economy in both Futures 1 and 2.

A longer war is detrimental for Ukraine's security and prosperity in both Futures 1 and 2. A longer war likely would mean a more economically devastated Ukraine, place greater strains on Europe's economy, and, in turn, reduce allies' willingness and ability to support Kyiv when the war was over.

In both Futures 1 and 2, there is a high risk of conflict along the LoC despite the differences in U.S. strategy. In both scenarios the combination of a reconquest-oriented Ukraine, an imperialistic Russia, and a weak ceasefire agreement increases the risk of renewed fighting along the LoC. That risk does not vary depending on the strategy the United States adopts.

This comparison suggests that taking steps to avoid a longer war, continuing to dissuade China from providing lethal combat support to Russia (which is less likely if the war ends sooner), and trying to help the parties to negotiate a more robust ceasefire are ways that the United States can promote its long-term interests while the war is ongoing. Moscow and Kyiv's motives are incredibly important to postwar stability, but are harder to influence through U.S. policy instruments.

Comparing the Implications of Different Strategies

As Figure 5.7 shows, the less hardline approach generally has more favorable implications for U.S. interests in both worlds (i.e., Future 2 is better than Future 1 and Future 4 is better than Future 3). To understand why, we note *distinctions* between futures that begin with the same conditions, but feature a different U.S. strategy.

The U.S. Position in the Global Distribution of Power

Earlier in this chapter, we detailed why, perhaps counterintuitively, the less hardline approach could strengthen U.S. relative power over the course

FIGURE 5.7

Summary of Implications for U.S. Interests

Interests		Future 1: Pervasive Instability	Future 2: Localized Instability	Future 3: Cold War 2.0	Future 4: Cold Peace
U.S. position in the global distribution of power	U.S. assured retaliation capability				
	Distribution of power in Europe	✓	✓✓	✓✓✓	✓✓✓✓
	Distribution of power in Asia	✕✕✕	✕✕	✕✕✕	✕
Avoiding a major power conflict	Risk of U.S.-Russia conventional conflict	✕✕✕✕	✕✕	✕✕✕	✕
	Risk of U.S.-Russia nuclear conflict	✕✕✕	✕✕	✕✕✕✕	✕
	Risk of U.S.-China nuclear conflict	✕✕✕	✕✕	✕✕✕	✕
Strength of the U.S. economy		✕✕✕✕	✕✕✕	✕✕✕	✕
Ukraine's security and prosperity	Ukraine's ability to defend itself	✕✕✕		✓✓✓	✓✓✓✓
	Risk of conflict recurrence	✕✕✕✕	✕✕	✕✕	✕
	Ukraine's economy and democracy	✕✕✕✕	✕✕✕	✕✕	✕
Minimizing conflict risk in other non-NATO former Soviet states		✕✕✕✕	✕✕	✕✕✕	✓

NOTE: The figure shows comparisons with pre-war trends, except for Ukraine's security and prosperity, which are compared across the four futures. For each measure or dimension of each measure, we rank the futures from most favorable (dark green, more checkmarks) to the United States to neutral (blank gray cells) to least favorable (dark red, more crosses). See text for a discussion of assumptions and uncertainties associated with these assessments.

of the postwar decade in both Europe and Asia. The material balance of power in Europe is not significantly affected by the less hardline approach in Futures 2 and 4 because the drawdown of U.S. forces and lower political tensions also temper Russia's investments in preparations for war with NATO. Moreover, in both postwar worlds, the less hardline approach leads to greater NATO cohesion and creates fewer pressures pushing Russia and China to form a de facto alliance. Assuming a fixed defense budget, the United States also has more resources available for the Indo-Pacific by adopting the less hardline approach toward Russia, which calls for fewer U.S. resources devoted to Europe.

Avoiding a Major Power Conflict

In both postwar worlds, the risk of a major power conflict is greater when the United States adopts the hardline approach than when it takes the less hardline approach. The hardline strategy leads to dynamics that can raise the risk of conflict, such as higher political tensions, increased chances for misperceptions about intentions, and crisis instability. Moreover, the hardline strategy is not likely to make deterrence in Europe more effective because NATO's military advantages are already so significant. In addition, the policies toward Ukraine that the United States adopts under the hardline approach (e.g., enabling an offensive maneuver capability, promoting integration with NATO) could make a second Russia-Ukraine war more likely, which, in turn, would raise the risk of Russia-NATO conflict. The probability of a major power war would still be low in an absolute sense if the United States implemented a hardline policy, but given the tremendous consequences of such an outcome, this risk should factor into U.S. decisionmaking.

Strength of the U.S. Economy

The less hardline approach would likely lead to marginally better economic outcomes for the United States. The less hardline U.S. approach is associated with lower risk of another Russia-Ukraine war and less global economic fragmentation in the postwar decade in both worlds. Therefore, the forces dragging on growth would be weaker than if the United States were to adopt a hardline approach.

Ukraine's Security and Prosperity

The less hardline U.S. approach would likely strengthen Ukraine's security and prosperity, because it is associated with a lower risk of conflict recurrence. The U.S. adoption of a porcupine model for its military assistance leaves Ukraine less vulnerable to future Russian attacks and better able to defend the territory it holds in Future 2 (compared with Future 1) and in Future 4 (compared with Future 3). Security improvements should, in turn, promote more investment in Ukraine and lead to more economic growth. Major Western European allies' likely preference for a Ukrainian defensive posture could lead them to provide greater economic aid if Kyiv adopts such a posture. The trade-off for Ukraine is that the porcupine strategy, which is the focus of the less hardline approach to military assistance, would not be ideally suited to retaking occupied territory in the event of a future war.

Minimizing Conflict Risk in Other Non-NATO Former Soviet States

Greater U.S. security cooperation and efforts to rollback Russian influence in other non-NATO states along Russia's periphery as part of a hardline U.S. strategy could sharpen Moscow's encirclement fears and thus increase the risk of conflict in this area compared with the less hardline strategy. A less hardline U.S. approach could leave these countries somewhat more vulnerable to Russian interference. However, Russia will likely always have some ability to influence; avoiding creation of incentives for armed intervention might be a more effective way to limit its consequences.

CHAPTER 6

Conclusion

In this report, we generate and compare alternative futures for the decade after the Russia-Ukraine war ends. We do so by simplifying very complex phenomena—the outcome of the war, the international environment, U.S. strategic choices—to highlight the most important considerations and trade-offs for U.S. policymakers.

Despite being systematic, futures analyses like the one we present here have important limitations. By definition, futures analysis is not predictive or comprehensive. We make no claim that one outcome is more likely than others. Moreover, although we ground our assessment of each future in the existing literature, there are many plausible futures beyond those that we consider here. We also conduct high-level assessments on many variables, from the risk of another war to economic effects. More-detailed analyses could be done on each of these individually. Despite the limitations of a structured futures approach, it is an important tool for evaluating postwar strategic options.

In the following sections, we offer observations based on what we learned from this exercise rather than specific policy recommendations.

Analytical Observations

A Longer, More Violent War Would Lock in Adverse Consequences for U.S. Interests

Unsurprisingly, our analysis indicates that the outcome of the war will have enduring effects on U.S. interests in the postwar decade. (It is worth underscoring that vertical or horizontal escalation of the war would have outsized effects on U.S. interests. We did not include escalation in our futures analysis precisely because it would have such an outsized impact.) Our analysis shows that a less favorable war outcome produces worse outcomes for U.S. interests at the end of that decade regardless of what Washington does in the postwar period. In other words, U.S. postwar strategy can at best mitigate the negative effects of a bad situation. For example, a longer war could significantly undermine Ukraine's postwar recovery. Possible effects include a less prosperous Ukraine with less ability to provide for its own defense and a sluggish European economy, which could, in turn, reduce postwar support to Ukraine and hurt trade with the United States and thus U.S. growth.

The United States May Be Able to Influence the Conflict Outcome to Promote Its Long-Term Postwar Interests

U.S. policy since February 2022 has been focused on using assistance and training to facilitate Ukrainian territorial gains. But U.S. policymakers should not lose sight of how wartime policies affect U.S. interests over the longer term. Of course, the United States cannot determine the outcome of the war on its own; its decisions will never have the same impact as those of the two combatants. But the United States does have policy options to try to affect the trajectory of the conflict and, specifically, to catalyze an end to the fighting in the shorter term. As we detail in the companion study to this report, the United States can take steps that could address key obstacles to negotiations, such as by offering security commitments to Ukraine or conditional sanctions relief to Russia.[1]

U.S. Policy During and After the War Can Reduce the Risk of Russia-Ukraine Conflict Recurrence

Another Russia-Ukraine conflict in decade after the war will be a distinct possibility—maybe even a likely outcome, given the degree of tensions and mutual grievances. Avoiding such an outcome will be an important priority for the United States. While the possibility of conflict recurrence will

---

[1] For a more detailed discussion of these connections, see Charap and Priebe, 2023.

depend on many factors, including Russia and Ukraine's postwar intentions, both wartime and postwar U.S. policy can have an impact.

First, using U.S. influence to encourage a nearer-term end to the current war would likely leave Ukraine in a better position to deter a future Russian invasion. The longer the war goes on, the greater the combat losses and economic impact. If the conflict ends sooner, Ukraine has greater chance of a more robust economic recovery, which will provide the long-term basis for rebuilding and sustaining its defenses. With stronger defenses, in turn, Russia will be less optimistic that it can achieve its goals through another invasion and thus would be less likely to attack.

Second, during and after the war, Washington can encourage Kyiv to adopt a porcupine posture. By focusing exclusively on optimizing its force for defending the territory that Ukraine already holds, the porcupine force planning concept should put Ukraine in a better position to defend against another attack (rather than expending resources on offensive maneuver capabilities for reconquest), thus increasing the country's ability to deter another Russian invasion. Russia would also be less likely to preventively attack Ukraine to attrit its capabilities if Moscow saw Kyiv postured for defense rather than offense. Additionally, Ukraine would be less likely to launch a war to retake occupied territory than if it had U.S.-provided capabilities designed for that purpose.

Finally, at the very end of the war, the United States could also use its influence to promote a more robust ceasefire agreement. Such an agreement, when compared with a weak ceasefire, would reduce the risk of another war. Studies have found that a well-crafted ceasefire has an independent effect on the likelihood of conflict recurrence. Such ceasefires can create confidence between recent belligerents about intentions, thus avoiding potential spiral dynamics. Of course, if one side is determined to fight another war no matter the costs, no ceasefire agreement can stop it. But a robust agreement can reduce the risk of breakdown through other pathways, such as those involving mutual suspicions and misinterpretations.

A Hardline Postwar U.S. Strategy Could Make Conflict with Russia More, Not Less, Likely

In Chapter 5, we describe multiple pathways to U.S.-Russia conflict and discuss how these conflict risks vary across the futures. We find that the two futures featuring hardline strategies produce more U.S. and NATO-Russia conflict risk in the postwar decade compared with those futures in which the United States adopts a less hardline approach.

In Futures 1 and 3, a weaker Russia responds belligerently to a U.S. buildup in Europe and political competition in post-Soviet Eurasia. An escalatory spiral could result, one that increases the possibility that misperception or a feeling of inevitable conflict could lead either NATO or Russia to launch a first strike.

A Russia-NATO conflict in the postwar period is less likely to result from opportunistic Russian aggression against an ally than it was before the war, given the significant diminution of Russian capabilities during the war. Even during the war, when Russia had ample reason to retaliate against NATO for arming its enemy, it did not, which suggests that NATO's deterrent effect is already strong. In the postwar period, with that motive diminished, it is unlikely that a weakened, isolated Russia will undertake an opportunistic war against the United States or a U.S. ally given the risks of conflict with a much more powerful alliance. A small reduction in forward-deployed U.S. forces is unlikely to change that assessment. In other words, it is not clear that a hardline U.S. policy would "buy" the United States much more deterrence against an opportunistic attack on a NATO ally. That said, even if Russia does not intend to attack, NATO needs forces and associated plans to address the contingency of a conflict with Moscow because there are other pathways to a NATO-Russia conflict, as we discussed in Chapter 5.

There is a similar dynamic at the strategic level. The United States and the Soviet Union, and later, Russia, have a long history of managing and controlling nuclear escalation risks. However, the current war has shattered bilateral relations and narrowed the space for future legally binding treaties, such as the NST. There will thus be more risks in the postwar period than before the war regardless. However, a hardline U.S. approach—i.e., refusal to engage in arms control, nuclear buildup, and the deployment of systems affecting strategic stability (e.g., BMD)—could increase those risks. As with regional contingencies, we find that Russia is deterred from attacking the

United States even under the less hardline policies. Therefore, we see greater conflict risk and no deterrence benefit from the hardline approach.

This Assessment Assumes That U.S.-Russia Conflict Would Result from Moscow's Assertive Responses to Hardline Policies, Not Opportunistic Aggression

Some analysts and policymakers would object to the previous finding, and instead draw a straight line between a tougher stance toward Russia and a reduction in the risk of war. This view assumes that U.S. policies, such as conventional and nuclear force posture enhancements, signal resolve and thus deter an opportunistic Russia from aggression against the United States and its NATO allies.

Our assessment of the conflict risk associated with the hardline strategy stems from two core assumptions about Russian behavior: that Moscow is deterred from an opportunistic attack on NATO but will respond assertively to a U.S. hardline strategy rather than accept it without contestation. These assertive responses could increase the risk of U.S.-Russia conflict through other pathways than opportunistic aggression.

As discussed previously, we assess that the hardline policy strategy produces little additional benefit in the futures because NATO, the United States, and its allies already have a strong deterrent against an opportunistic Russian attack. This judgment rests on the assumption that Russia's risk tolerance—particularly its willingness to risk a war with the United States and its NATO allies—will be relatively similar to what it is as of this writing. In other words, Russia is not inclined to undertake an opportunistic war of aggression against the United States or its allies. Indeed, even at the time of this writing, when Russia has a clear motive to attack NATO to stem the flow of weapons to Ukraine, it has refrained from doing so.

However, the lesson of Russia's hugely risky gamble in February 2022—one that was not anticipated before the preparations became obvious—is that the Kremlin's intentions can change in unexpected ways. Therefore, the United States should continue to monitor for changes in Russia's risk tolerance. For example, if it seems that Russia's willingness to risk attacking a NATO member-state is growing, then an increase in NATO forces in the area might have more benefit in preventing certain types of conflict. In other words, if Russia becomes much more risk-acceptant than it has ever been historically, a hardline approach may increase NATO's ability to deter Russian aggression.

The conflict risks in Futures 1 and 3 are driven by the assumption that Russia will respond assertively to hardline elements of U.S. strategy. For example, we assume that Russia will take steps to counter the U.S. nuclear buildup and rejection of arms control, and that these steps will lead to greater instability. These assertive responses to U.S. policy and any subsequent action-reaction cycle with the United States would increase the risk of misperception about intentions. Although we assume that Moscow is deterred from an opportunistic war against NATO, we assess that Russia might find it difficult to back down in an escalatory spiral. In the extreme, it might even take the risk of an anticipatory attack, if it saw (1) its survival on the line, (2) war as increasingly inevitable, and (3) first strike advantages. These assumptions are grounded in both the recent history of Russian foreign policy and the general international relations literature. However, Russia's postwar weakness (or some other factor) could result in a different pattern of responses to U.S. hardline policies. If Moscow did not counter U.S. hardline policies as expected, the costs and risks associated with them would be lower than we anticipate in this report.

Closer Russia-China Ties May Already Be Locked In

Past RAND research has documented how concerns about U.S. policy brought Russia and China closer together after Russia's invasion of Crimea in 2014.[2] The war has so far deepened these ties. A major Russian escalation, such as nuclear use or attack on a NATO member-state, could give China second thoughts regarding its support to Russia. But absent such an extreme outcome, the main driver of Russia-China cooperation—U.S. power and a grand strategy that involves deep military engagement in Europe, Asia, and other key regions—is likely to remain in place after the war.

Given what we know about Russian and Soviet responses to less hardline U.S. approaches in the past, we expect that a limited U.S. accommodation

---

[2] Radin et al., 2021.

will have only a modest effect on Russian threat perceptions.[3] Such a policy might not push Russia and China as closely together as a hardline U.S. policy toward Russia might. But it is unlikely that a limited less hardline approach will significantly weaken Russia-China ties from their wartime height.

Postwar Disagreements with Core Western European NATO Allies Could Have Significant Effects on U.S. Interests

Current U.S. strategy in Europe places a high value on alliance unity. NATO allies have presented a largely united front on policy since Russia's full-scale invasion began, but this cohesion could come under strain during the postwar period. Behind the facade of outward unity, even during the war, allies have voiced divergent views about the efficacy and risks of different policies. For example, Germany has been more cautious about stepping up support to Ukraine than Poland. The pressures of war, however, have led allies to find solutions to these differences. In the postwar period, these pressures will relax, and the divisions among allies that have been common in peacetime will likely reemerge.

After the war, a hardline U.S. approach to a Russia that is behaving less belligerently may encounter pushback from allies such as France, Italy, and Germany. Conversely, some Eastern European allies would likely oppose a less hardline U.S. approach under any circumstances—at least those imagined in this report.

However, as we detailed in Chapters 4 and 5, some disagreements may be more problematic for the United States than others. Eastern European allies are more dependent on the United States for their security. Therefore, they are more likely to remain committed to NATO and collective defense than Western European allies in light of policy differences with the United States.

---

[3] Priebe, Frederick, Evans, et al., 2023.

Conclusion

This alternative futures analysis suggests that U.S. policy choices both during the Russia-Ukraine war and immediately after can have significant effects on long-term U.S. interests. With so much uncertainty about the trajectory of the war as of this writing, the policy debate is likely to focus on immediate and urgent decisions rather than postwar planning. But putting off these considerations could be counterproductive for the United States. Our analysis indicates that wartime choices could shape the postwar world; not taking these longer-term factors into consideration could lead to missed opportunities to shape the postwar environment. Moreover, the choices that will have to be made in the immediate aftermath of the war can have ripple effects on many long-term U.S. interests, and these effects are not straightforward. Policymakers thus need time long before the war ends to consider these choices. We hope that this analysis can help start that process of long-term planning.

Abbreviations

BMD	ballistic missile defense
C4ISR	command, control, communications, computers, intelligence, surveillance, and reconnaissance
CFE	Treaty on Conventional Armed Forces in Europe
EU	European Union
GDP	gross domestic product
ICBM	intercontinental ballistic missile
INF	Intermediate-Range Nuclear Forces Treaty
LoC	line of contact
NATO	North Atlantic Treaty Organization
NSNW	nonstrategic nuclear weapon
NST	New START Treaty
OECD	Organisation for Economic Co-operation and Development
ROK	Republic of Korea
SSBN	ballistic missile submarine
UAF	Ukrainian Armed Forces

References

Akinci, Ozge, and Paolo Pesenti, "Do Economic Crises in Europe Affect the U.S.? Some Lessons from the Past Three Decades," *Liberty Street Economics*, May 31, 2023.

Arthur, David, and F. Matthew Woodward, *Long-Term Implications of the 2023 Future Years Defense Program*, Congressional Budget Office, January 2023.

Aza, Hibai Arbide, and Miguel Gonzalez, "US Offered Disarmament Measures to Russia in Exchange for Deescalation of Military Threat in Ukraine," *El País*, February 2, 2022.

Baker, Sinéad, and Jake Epstein, "Front-Line NATO Allies Worry They Could Be Next After Russia's Invasion of Ukraine and Are Getting Ready for a Fight," *Business Insider*, April 23, 2023.

Barrass, Gordon, "Able Archer 83: What Were the Soviets Thinking?" *Survival*, Vol. 58, No. 6, December 2016–January 2017.

Bell, Mark S., and Julia Macdonald, "How to Think About Nuclear Crises (February 2019)," *Texas National Security Review*, Vol. 2, No. 2, February 2019.

Biden, Joseph R., Jr., "Remarks by President Biden on Russia," White House, April 15, 2021.

Biden, Joseph R., Jr., *National Security Strategy*, White House, October 12, 2022.

Binnendijk, Anika, and Miranda Priebe, *An Attack Against Them All? Drivers of Decisions to Contribute to NATO Collective Defense*, RAND Corporation, RR-2964-OSD, 2019. As of November 21, 2023:
https://www.rand.org/pubs/research_reports/RR2964.html

Boose, Donald W., Jr., "The Korean War Truce Talks: A Study in Conflict Termination," *Parameters*, Vol. 30, No. 1, Spring 2000.

Brooks, Linton F., "The End of Arms Control?" *Daedalus*, Vol. 149, No. 2, Spring 2020.

Bruhin, Jonas, Rolf Scheufele, and Yannic Stucki, "The Economic Impact of Russia's Invasion of Ukraine on European Countries—a SVAR Approach," SSRN Working Paper No. 04-2024, September 22, 2023.

Cable, Jonathan, "Worsening Euro Zone Business Downturn Reignites Recession Fears," *Reuters*, July 24, 2023.

Charap, Samuel, "An Unwinnable War: Washington Needs an Endgame in Ukraine," *Foreign Affairs*, Vol. 102, No. 4, July–August 2023.

Charap, Samuel, and Timothy J. Colton, *Everyone Loses: The Ukraine Crisis and the Ruinous Contest for Post-Soviet Eurasia*, Routledge, 2017.

Charap, Samuel, John J. Drennan, Luke Griffith, Edward Geist, and Brian G. Carlson, *Mitigating Challenges to U.S.-Russia Strategic Stability*, RAND Corporation, RR-A1094-1, 2022. As of November 21, 2023: https://www.rand.org/pubs/research_reports/RRA1094-1.html

Charap, Samuel, Edward Geist, Bryan Frederick, John J. Drennan, Nathan Chandler, and Jennifer Kavanagh, *Russia's Military Interventions: Patterns, Drivers, and Signposts*, RAND Corporation, RR-A444-3, 2021. As of January 2, 2024: https://www.rand.org/pubs/research_reports/RRA444-3.html

Charap, Samuel, Alice Lynch, John J. Drennan, Dara Massicot, and Giacomo Persi Paoli, *A New Approach to Conventional Arms Control in Europe: Addressing the Security Challenges of the 21st Century*, RAND Corporation, RR-4346, 2020. As of November 21, 2023: https://www.rand.org/pubs/research_reports/RR4346.html

Charap, Samuel, Dara Massicot, Miranda Priebe, Alyssa Demus, Clint Reach, Mark Stalczynski, Eugeniu Han, and Lynn E. Davis, *Russian Grand Strategy: Rhetoric and Reality*, RAND Corporation, RR-4238-A, 2021. As of November 21, 2023: https://www.rand.org/pubs/research_reports/RR4238.html

Charap, Samuel, and Miranda Priebe, *Avoiding a Long War: U.S. Policy and the Trajectory of the Russia-Ukraine Conflict*, RAND Corporation, PE-A2510-1, 2023. As of November 21, 2023: https://www.rand.org/pubs/perspectives/PEA2510-1.html

Chekinov, Sergei, and Sergei Bogdanov, "The Essence and Content of the Evolving Notion of War in the 21st Century," *Military Thought*, Vol. 1, 2017.

Chernenko, Elena, "Vladimir Putin's Letter Reached the Right Addressee," *Kommersant*, November 27, 2019.

Clauset, Aaron, "Trends and Fluctuations in the Severity of Interstate Wars," *Science Advances*, Vol. 4, No. 2, February 2018.

Cohen, Patricia, "Russia's Economy Is Increasingly Structured Around Its War in Ukraine," *New York Times*, October 9, 2023.

Colton, Timothy, "Ukraine and Russia: War and Political Regimes," *Journal of Democracy*, Vol. 33, No. 4, October 2022.

Copeland, Dale C., *The Origins of Major War*, Cornell University Press, 2000.

Copp, Tara, "How Ukraine War Has Shaped US Planning for a China Conflict," *Associated Press*, February 16, 2023.

Council of Europe, "G7 Joint Declaration of Support for Ukraine," July 12, 2023.

Creedon, Madelyn R., Jon L. Kyl, Marshall S. Billingslea, Gloria C. Duffy, Rose E. Gottemoeller, Lisa E. Gordon-Hagerty, Rebeccah L. Heinrichs, John E. Hyten, Robert M. Scher, Matthew H. Kroenig, Franklin C. Miller, and Leonor A. Tomero, *America's Strategic Posture: The Final Report of the Congressional Commission on the Strategic Posture of the United States*, Institute for Defense Analyses, October 2023.

Cunningham, Fiona S., and M. Taylor Fravel, "Assuring Assured Retaliation: China's Nuclear Posture and U.S.-China Strategic Stability," *International Security*, Vol. 40, No. 2, Fall 2015.

Cunningham, Fiona S., and M. Taylor Fravel, "Dangerous Confidence? Chinese Views on Nuclear Escalation," *International Security*, Vol. 44, No. 2, Fall 2019.

"The Curious Case of Russia's Missing Air Force," *The Economist*, March 8, 2022.

Davies, Shawn, Therése Pettersson, and Magnus Öberg, "Organized Violence 1989–2022, and the Return of Conflict Between States," *Journal of Peace Research*, Vol. 60, No. 4, July 2023.

Demarais, Agathe, "What Does 'De-Risking' Actually Mean?" *Foreign Policy*, August 23, 2023.

Democratic Initiatives Foundation, *Analytical Report Based on the Results of War, Peace, Victory, and Future Survey*, August 16, 2023.

Deudney, Daniel, and G. John Ikenberry, "The Unravelling of the Cold War Settlement," *Survival*, Vol. 51, No. 6, December 2009–January 2010.

Disney, Richard, "What Is the Current State of the Russian Economy Under Sanctions?" Economics Observatory, April 27, 2023.

Dvorkin, Vladimir, "Preserving Strategic Stability Amid U.S.-Russian Confrontation," Carnegie Moscow Center, February 2019.

European Council, "Infographic—Impact of Sanctions on the Russian Economy," last reviewed October 12, 2023.

Evans, Alexandra T., *Alternative Futures Following a Great Power War, Vol. 2: Supporting Material on Historical Great Power Wars*, RAND Corporation, RR-A591-2, 2023. As of November 29, 2023:
https://www.rand.org/pubs/research_reports/RRA591-2.html

Eversden, Andrew, "Missile Defense Chief 'Confident' Poland's Aegis Ashore Ready in 2023," *Breaking Defense*, August 12, 2022.

Faulconbridge, Guy, "Blood and Billions: The Cost of Russia's War in Ukraine," Reuters, August 23, 2023.

Fearon, James D., "Two States, Two Types, Two Actions," *Security Studies*, Vol. 20, No. 3, 2011.

Feickert, Andrew, *The U.S. Army's Long-Range Hypersonic Weapon (LRHW)*, Congressional Research Service, IF11991, updated September 15, 2023a.

Feickert, Andrew, *The U.S. Army's Strategic Mid-Range Fires (SMRF) System (Formerly Mid-Range Capabilities [MRC] System)*, Congressional Research Service, IF12135, updated November 28, 2023b.

Felbermayr, Gabriel, Hendrik Mahlkow, and Alexander Sandkamp, "Cutting Through the Value Chain: The Long-Run Effects of Decoupling the East from the West," *Empirica: Journal of European Economics*, Vol. 50, No. 1, February 2023.

Fix, Liana, and Michael Kimmage, "How China Could Save Putin's War in Ukraine: The Logic—and Consequences—of Chinese Military Support for Russia," *Foreign Affairs*, April 26, 2023.

Fortna, Virginia Page, "Scraps of Paper? Agreements and the Durability of Peace," *International Organization*, Vol. 57, No. 2, Spring 2003.

Fortna, Virginia Page, *Peace Time: Cease-Fire Agreements and the Durability of Peace*, Princeton University Press, 2004a.

Fortna, Virginia Page, "Interstate Peacekeeping: Causal Mechanisms and Empirical Effects," *World Politics*, Vol. 56, No. 4, July 2004b.

Frederick, Bryan, Samuel Charap, Scott Boston, Stephen J. Flanagan, Michael J. Mazarr, Jennifer D. P. Moroney, and Karl P. Mueller, *Pathways to Russian Escalation Against NATO from the Ukraine War*, RAND Corporation, PE-A1971-1, 2022. As of November 29, 2023: https://www.rand.org/pubs/perspectives/PEA1971-1.html

Frederick, Bryan, Mark Cozad, and Alexandra Stark, *Escalation in the War in Ukraine: Lessons Learned and Risks for the Future*, RAND Corporation, RR-A2807-1, 2023. As of November 29, 2023: https://www.rand.org/pubs/research_reports/RRA2807-1.html

"Full Transcript: Biden's Speech on Israel-Hamas and Russia-Ukraine Wars," *New York Times*, October 19, 2023.

Gamio, Lazaro, and Ana Swanson, "How Russia Pays for War," *New York Times*, October 30, 2022.

Harris, Bryant, "Document Reveals $14 Billion Backlog of US Defense Transfers to Taiwan," *Defense News*, April 14, 2022.

Heisbourg, François, "How to End a War: Some Historical Lessons for Ukraine," *Survival*, Vol. 65, No. 4, August–September 2023.

Hill, Fiona, and Angela Stent, "The World Putin Wants: How Distortions About the Past Feed Delusions About the Future," *Foreign Affairs*, Vol. 101, No. 5, September–October 2022.

Hollinger, Peggy, "Russia's War on Ukraine Holds Still More Pain for European Business," *Financial Times*, August 9, 2023.

Hruby, Jill, *Russia's New Nuclear Weapon Delivery Systems: An Open-Source Technical Review*, Nuclear Threat Initiative, November 13, 2019.

Ikenberry, G. John, *After Victory: Institutions, Strategic Restraint, and the Rebuilding of Order After Major Wars*, Princeton University Press, 2001.

Inbar, Efraim, and Eitan Shamir, "'Mowing the Grass': Israel's Strategy for Protracted Intractable Conflict," *Journal of Strategic Studies*, Vol. 37, No. 1, 2014.

International Monetary Fund, *World Economic Outlook: Navigating Global Divergences*, October 1, 2023.

Janzen, Joe, and Carl Zulauf, "The Russia-Ukraine War and Changes in Ukraine Corn and Wheat Supply: Impacts on Global Agricultural Markets," *Farmdoc Daily*, Vol. 13, No. 34, February 24, 2023.

Jervis, Robert, *Perception and Misperception in International Politics*, Princeton University Press, 1976.

Jones, Marc, "JPMorgan Flags Some Signs of Emerging De-Dollarisation," *Reuters*, June 5, 2023.

Kearn, David, Jr., *Reassessing U.S. Nuclear Strategy*, Cambria Press, 2019.

Kirchberger, Sarah, "Obstacles and Breakthroughs in China's Defense Technological Development : China's Undersea Warfare," testimony before the U.S.-China Economic and Security Review Commission, April 13, 2023.

Kirshner, Jonathan, "Rationalist Explanations for War?" *Security Studies*, Vol. 10, No. 1, Autumn 2000.

Kluge, Janis, "The West Shouldn't Underestimate Russia's Resilience," *Moscow Times*, September 15, 2023.

Kluth, Andreas, "Ukraine's Future Isn't German or Israeli but Korean," Bloomberg, August 30, 2023.

Krastev, Ivan, and Mark Leonard, "Peace Versus Justice: The Coming European Split over the War in Ukraine," ECFR Policy Brief, No. 452, June 15, 2022.

Kristensen, Hans M., Matt Korda, and Eliana Johns, "Nuclear Notebook: Russian Nuclear Weapons, 2023," *Bulletin of the Atomic Scientists*, Vol. 79, No. 3, 2023.

Kristensen, Hans M., Matt Korda, Eliana Johns, and Kate Kohn, "Status of World Nuclear Forces," Federation of American Scientists, March 31, 2023.

Kroenig, Matthew, "Nuclear Superiority and the Balance of Resolve: Explaining Nuclear Crisis Outcomes," *International Organization*, Vol. 67, No. 1, Winter 2013.

Leromain, Elsa, and Marcus Biermann, "How Has the Russian Invasion of Ukraine Affected Global Financial Markets?" Economics Observatory, May 25, 2023.

Levy, Jack S., "Preventive War: Concept and Propositions," *International Interactions*, Vol. 37, No. 1, 2011.

Levy, Jack S., and Joseph R. Gochal, "Democracy and Preventive War: Israel and the 1956 Sinai Campaign," *Security Studies*, Vol. 11, No. 2, Autumn 2001.

Lieber, Keir A., and Daryl G. Press, "The Rise of U.S. Nuclear Primacy," *Foreign Affairs*, Vol. 85, No. 2, March–April 2006.

Lieber, Keir A., and Daryl G. Press, "The New Era of Counterforce: Technological Change and the Future of Nuclear Deterrence," *International Security*, Vol. 41, No. 4, Spring 2017.

Lin, Bonny, "The China-Russia Axis Takes Shape," *Foreign Policy*, September 11, 2023.

Logan, David C., "The Nuclear Balance Is What States Make of It," *International Security*, Vol. 46, No. 4, Spring 2022.

Lührmann, Anna, and Bryan Rooney, "Autocratization by Decree: States of Emergency and Democratic Decline," *Comparative Politics*, Vol. 53, No. 4, July 2021.

Malkasian, Carter, "The Korea Model: Why an Armistice Offers the Best Hope for Peace in Ukraine," *Foreign Affairs*, Vol. 102, No. 4, July–August 2023.

Masters, Jonathan, and Will Merrow, "Nuclear Weapons in Europe: Mapping U.S. and Russian Deployments," Council on Foreign Relations, March 30, 2023.

Matray, James I., "Korea's War at 60: A Survey of the Literature," *Cold War History*, Vol. 11, No. 1, 2011.

Medcalf, Rory, Katherine Mansted, Stephan Frühling, and James Goldrick, eds., *The Future of the Undersea Deterrent: A Global Survey*, Australian National University, National Security College, Indo-Pacific Strategy Series, February 2020.

Merchant, Nomaan, Ellen Knickmeyer, Zeke Miller, and Tara Copp, "US Announces $345 Million Military Aid Package for Taiwan," Associated Press, July 29, 2023.

Ministry of Foreign Affairs of the Republic of Poland, "Statement of the Minister of Foreign Affairs of the Republic of Poland in Connection with the Statement by the US Secretary of State on Providing Airplanes to Ukraine," August 3, 2022.

Mueller, Karl P., Jasen J. Castillo, Forrest E. Morgan, Negeen Pegahi, and Brian Rosen, *Striking First: Preemptive and Preventive Attack in U.S. National Security Policy*, RAND Corporation, MG-403-AF, 2006. As of November 29, 2023:
https://www.rand.org/pubs/monographs/MG403.html

Murray, William S., "Revisiting Taiwan's Defense Strategy," *Naval War College Review*, Vol. 61, No. 3, Summer 2008.

NATO—*See* North Atlantic Treaty Organization.

Nephew, Richard, "The Hard Part: The Art of Sanctions Relief," *Washington Quarterly*, Vol. 41, No. 2, 2018.

North Atlantic Treaty Organization, *North Atlantic Treaty*, signed at Washington, D.C., 1949.

North Atlantic Treaty Organization, "Final Communiqué," statement at the meeting of the North Atlantic Council Defence Ministers Session, M-NAC(DM)-3(96)172, December 18, 1996.

North Atlantic Treaty Organization, "Bucharest Summit Declaration," April 3, 2008.

OECD—*See* Organisation for Economic Co-operation and Development.

Organisation for Economic Co-operation and Development, *Economic Outlook, Interim Report*, March 1, 2023.

Pérez, Louis A., Jr., "The Meaning of the Maine: Causation and the Historiography of the Spanish-American War," *Pacific Historical Review*, Vol. 58, No. 3, August 1989.

Posen, Barry R., *Restraint: A New Foundation for U.S. Grand Strategy*, Cornell University Press, 2014.

President of Russia, "Statement by Vladimir Putin on Additional Steps to De-Escalate the Situation in Europe in the Context of the Termination of the Intermediate-Range Nuclear Forces (INF) Treaty," October 26, 2020.

Press, Daryl G., *Calculating Credibility: How Leaders Assess Military Threats*, Cornell University Press, 2005.

Pressman, Jeremy, *Warring Friends: Alliance Restraint in International Politics*, Cornell University Press, 2008.

Priebe, Miranda, Bryan Frederick, Anika Binnendijk, Alexandra T. Evans, Karl P. Mueller, Cortez A. Cooper III, James Benkowski, Asha Clark, and Stephanie Anne Pillion, *Alternative Futures Following a Great Power War,* Vol. 1: *Scenarios, Findings, and Recommendations,* RAND Corporation, RR-A591-1, 2023. As of November 29, 2023:
https://www.rand.org/pubs/research_reports/RRA591-1.html

Priebe, Miranda, Bryan Frederick, Alexandra T. Evans, Samuel Charap, Gabrielle Tarini, and Bryan Rooney, *Future U.S. Peacetime Policy Toward Russia: Exploring the Benefits and Costs of a Less-Hardline Approach,* RAND Corporation, RR-A1862-1, 2023. As of November 29, 2023:
https://www.rand.org/pubs/research_reports/RRA1862-1.html

Quackenbush, Stephen L, "The Problem with Accidental War," *Conflict Management and Peace Science,* Vol. 40, No. 6, November 2023.

Radin, Andrew, Andrew Scobell, Elina Treyger, J. D. Williams, Logan Ma, Howard J. Shatz, Sean M. Zeigler, Eugeniu Han, and Clint Reach, *China-Russia Cooperation: Determining Factors, Future Trajectories, Implications for the United States,* RAND Corporation, RR-3067-A, 2021. As of November 29, 2023:
https://www.rand.org/pubs/research_reports/RR3067.html

Reiter, Dan, "Exploding the Powder Keg Myth: Preemptive Wars Almost Never Happen," *International Security,* Vol. 20, No. 2, Fall 1995.

Reporters Without Borders, "RSF's 2022 World Press Freedom Index: A New Era of Polarisation," May 3, 2022.

Rogoff, Kenneth, "The Long-Lasting Economic Shock of War," International Monetary Fund, March 2023.

Rooney, Bryan, Grant Johnson, Tobias Sytsma, and Miranda Priebe, *Does the U.S. Economy Benefit from U.S. Alliances and Forward Military Presence?* RAND Corporation, RR-A739-5, 2022. As of November 29, 2023:
https://www.rand.org/pubs/research_reports/RRA739-5.html

Roque, Ashley, "To Combat China, Pentagon Eyeing Multi-Year Munition Buys in FY24," *Breaking Defense,* March 13, 2023.

"Russia's Defense Chief Proposes Re-Establishing Moscow, Leningrad Military Districts," TASS, December 21, 2022.

Rustamova, Farida, "Ukraine's 10-Point Plan," *Faridaily* blog, March 29, 2022. As of November 29, 2023:
https://faridaily.substack.com/p/ukraines-10-point-plan

Saine, Cindy, "Biden Cites US Resolve in Facing Aggression from Russia and China," Voice of America, February 8, 2023.

Schelling, Thomas C., and Morton H. Halperin, *Strategy and Arms Control,* Pergamon-Brassey's, 1985.

Schweller, Randall L., "Domestic Structure and Preventive War: Are Democracies More Pacific?" *World Politics*, Vol. 44, No. 2, January 1992.

Sechser, Todd S., and Matthew Fuhrmann, "Crisis Bargaining and Nuclear Blackmail," *International Organization*, Vol. 67, No. 1, Winter 2013.

Snyder, Glenn H., "The Security Dilemma in Alliance Politics," *World Politics*, Vol. 36, No. 4, July 1984.

Snyder, Ryan, Benoît Pelopidas, Keir A. Lieber, and Daryl G. Press, "Correspondence: New Era or New Error? Technology and the Future of Deterrence," *International Security*, Vol. 43, No. 3, Winter 2018–2019.

Stueck, William, *The Korean War: An International History*, Princeton University Press, 1995.

Stueck, William, "Conclusion," in William Stueck, ed., *The Korean War in World History*, University Press of Kentucky, 2004.

Sullivan, Jake, "Remarks by National Security Advisor Jake Sullivan for the Arms Control Association (ACA) Annual Forum," June 2, 2023.

Talmadge, Caitlin, "Would China Go Nuclear? Assessing the Risk of Chinese Nuclear Escalation in a Conventional War with the United States," *International Security*, Vol. 41, No. 4, Spring 2017.

Trachtenberg, Marc, "The 'Accidental War' Question," February 14, 2000.

"Ukraine War: Putin Confirms First Nuclear Weapons Moved to Belarus," BBC News, June 17, 2023.

U.S. Department of Defense, *2022 Nuclear Posture Review*, 2022a.

U.S. Department of Defense, "Statement by Pentagon Press Secretary John F. Kirby on Security Assistance to Ukraine," March 8, 2022b.

U.S. Department of Defense, "Fact Sheet—U.S. Defense Contributions to Europe," June 29, 2022c.

U.S. Department of Defense, *Military and Security Developments Involving the People's Republic of China, Annual Report to Congress*, November 29, 2022d.

U.S. Department of Defense, Office of the General Counsel, *Department of Defense Law of War Manual*, updated 2016.

Van Evera, Stephen, *Causes of War: Structures of Power and the Roots of International Conflict*, Cornell University Press, 1999.

Warrick, Joby, "China Is Building More Than 100 New Missile Silos in Its Western Desert, Analysts Say," *Washington Post*, June 30, 2021.

Weisiger, Alex, and Keren Yarhi-Milo, "Revisiting Reputation: How Past Actions Matter in International Politics," *International Organization*, Vol. 69, No. 2, Spring 2015.

Werner, Suzanne, "The Precarious Nature of Peace: Resolving the Issues, Enforcing the Settlement, and Renegotiating the Terms," *American Journal of Political Science*, Vol. 43, No. 3, July 1999.

Wilkening, Dean A., "Strategic Stability Between the United States and Russia," in David Ochmanek and Michael Sulmeyer, eds., *Challenges in U.S. National Security Policy: A Festschrift Honoring Edward L. (Ted) Warner,* RAND Corporation, CP-765-RAS, 2014. As of November 29, 2023: https://www.rand.org/pubs/corporate_pubs/CP765.html

World Bank, *Ukraine Rapid Damage and Needs Assessment: February 2022– February 2023*, 2023.

Ziegler, Charles E., "A Crisis of Diverging Perspectives: U.S.-Russian Relations and the Security Dilemma," *Texas National Security Review*, Vol. 4, No. 1, Winter 2020–2021.

Milton Keynes UK
Ingram Content Group UK Ltd.
UKHW050237150424
441046UK00005B/18

9 781977 412836